BRITISH COLUMBIA PROVINCIAL MUSEUM

HANDBOOK No. 40

CRABS AND THEIR RELATIVES OF BRITISH COLUMBIA

Written and Illustrated
by
Josephine F. L. Hart

Province of British Columbia
Ministry of Provincial Secretary
and Government Services
Provincial Secretary

Published by the British Columbia Provincial Museum
Victoria

First Printing 1982

Canadian Cataloguing in Publication Data

Hart, Josephine F. L.
    Crabs and their relatives of British Columbia

    (Handbook / British Columbia Provincial Museum,
ISSN 0068-1628 ; no. 40)

    Bibliography: p.
    ISBN 0-7718-8314-5

    1. Crabs - British Columbia.   I. British Columbia
Provincial Museum.   II. Title.   III. Series: Handbook (British Columbia Provincial Museum) ; no. 40.

    QL444.M33H37   595.3'842'09711   C82-092226-9

ii

The Friends of the Provincial Museum
contributed generously toward the cost of printing
the colour illustrations (following page 60) in this book.

FOREWORD

This book is special for two reasons.

Dr. Hart has distilled many years of study into these pages. For scientist and beachcomber, and those of us between, she makes available here her knowledge from a life-long investigation of crabs found in the marine waters of British Columbia. These are waters rich in life, with an impressive abundance and variety of crabs, and now we have a species Who's Who for this well known group of armoured and lively creatures. The many of us that for many reasons are fascinated by the improbable forms of life in the sea can now watch crabs *and* put names on them. All it takes is a little study and some really seeing what we look at. Here Dr. Hart gives us 95 kinds to look for.

This handbook marks the 40 years that this popular series has served the people of British Columbia. In 1942, Handbook 1 began as a type-written, offset printed, edition of *Fifty Edible Plants of British Columbia* by George A. Hardy. That book was the brainchild of Dr. Clifford Carl, Director of this museum, who, in its foreword, stated it to be the first of a series ". . . dealing with various groups of the flora and fauna of the Province of British Columbia and may also include material relating to the native Indian tribes." For many years this series, with many titles in it written by Dr. Carl, has been the best and most popular such series on this continent. As I write, it contains 39 titles, most still in print.

It is entirely satisfying and appropriate that, after 40 years, the 40th title in this series begun by Dr. Carl is written by Dr. Josephine F. L. Hart, who is also Mrs. G. Clifford Carl.

R. Yorke Edwards
Director

ACKNOWLEDGEMENTS

The staff of the British Columbia Provincial Museum has been consistently helpful in the preparation of this book. In 1962, a grant (No. G21168) from the United States National Science Foundation provided necessary equipment, literature and free time for research. Without these advantages the project would not have been accomplished. I am indeed grateful for this assistance.

I have been fortunate to have seen alive the majority of the species described here. Intertidal species I could collect myself while subtidal presented difficulties. Therefore, I appreciate the opportunities given me to obtain specimens of deep-water species in British Columbia. These have been obtained from a number of sources in British Columbia and through gifts and loans from the United States. In British Columbia, collections were obtained from the dredging activities of several commercial draggers, expeditions by the staff of Government of Canada, Fisheries and Oceans (formerly the Fisheries Research Board of Canada) Pacific Biological Station at Departure Bay, Nanaimo, the University of Victoria's Biology Department and the British Columbia Provincial Museum in Victoria. Since I participated in only a few dredging expeditions, I am most appreciative of the help and the material given me by my colleagues, particularly D. B. Quayle, T. H. Butler and F. R. Bernard of the Nanaimo Station, A. R. Fontaine, D. V. Ellis and J. E. McInerney of the University of Victoria and A. E. Peden and P. Lambert of the British Columbia Provincial Museum. Sincere thanks are due also to individuals from various institutions in the United States: P. L. Illg and C. F. Nyblade of the University of Washington, Seattle; F. A. Chace, Jr. and R. B. Manning, Smithsonian Institution, Washington, D.C.; J. Haig and J. S. Garth, Allan Hancock Foundation, Los Angeles, California; and P. A. McLaughlin, Florida International University, Miami, Florida. The late B. A. Stevens, of Seattle and G. C. Carl of Victoria, encouraged and advised me in the early stages of this project.

Josephine F. L. Hart

CONTENTS

CONTENTS—*Continued*

CONTENTS—*Continued*

LIST OF FIGURES

LIST OF FIGURES—*Continued*

LIST OF FIGURES—*Continued*

LIST OF FIGURES—*Continued*

INTRODUCTION

He was round and he was flat;
and his eyes grew upon stalks;
and he walked sideways like this;
and he was covered with strong armour on his back.

Just So Stories
RUDYARD KIPLING

Everyone knows a 'crab'. Don't be a 'crab' (cranky), 'catch a crab' (while rowing a boat) or 'walk like a crab' (sideways). *Cancer,* Latin for crab, has been used for many years as the name of a constellation of stars, and also horoscopically (June 22 to July 22). The Tropic of Cancer is another ancient use of the term. *Cancer* originally was a general name for crabs, but now, scientifically, it refers only to one genus of crabs.

Crabs and their relatives (i.e., reptant decapod crustacea) live in a great variety of habitats. Marine species occupy zones from seashore to abyss and from the surface of the ocean down to the sea bottom substratum, which they may penetratre to depths of at least one metre. Other species live in fresh-water lakes and rivers. In British Columbia all are marine with the exception of the fresh-water crayfish *Pacifastacus*. In tropical areas terrestrial species occur and are often nocturnal, hiding in burrows or crevices during daylight. The females enter the water when their eggs are ready to hatch so that the larvae are aquatic and become terrestrial as juveniles.

Crabs and other decapod crustacea which are 'crawlers' are grouped together under the name Reptantia, or reptant, as opposed to the swimmers, or Natantia, which are the true shrimps and prawns. This book is concerned with the Reptantia only, a Suborder divided into three Sections: the Macrura, or 'large tails'; the Anomura, or 'asymmetrical tails'; and the Brachyura, or 'short tails'. It deals with all the known species of Reptantia in British Columbia.

In the waters off British Columbia the Macrura are represented by burrowing shrimps and possibly by the American lobster which has been introduced into British Columbia several times, apparently unsuccessfully. Lobsters thrive on the Atlantic coast of North America in a type of habitat that is not found on the Pacific coast. Other factors concerned

11

Fig. 1   Marine waters of British Columbia showing 200 m and 2000 m depth contours.

12

with ecology and especially predators appear to be detrimental to the introduction. Of the Anomura, some 50 species are known, comprising squat lobsters, porcelain crabs, hermit crabs, lithodid crabs and sand crabs. The Brachyura, or true crabs, include over 30 species.

There is an excellent account of these animals, entitled *Crustaceans*, by Waldo L. Schmitt (1965) which is unsurpassed. He gives an overall review of the Crustacea including much useful information for their study. Schmitt's book is a perfect introduction to the group. Since it was published many interesting results of work on decapod crustacea have been recorded. One concerns the early life history of the coconut crab, *Birgus latro* Linnaeus. The adults are a kind of hermit crab that lives on land, feeds on coconuts and which become very large. Their fat abdomen is well calcified dorsally and so they do not use a mollusc shell for protection as do most of their relatives. It was long known that the larval development took place in the sea because the females enter the water when the eggs are ready to hatch. When the larval stages were reared in the laboratory, it was discovered that the juvenile stages use shells like typical hermit crabs. They then become terrestrial and, when they have grown and have a carapace length of 18–20 mm, the shell is discarded and the colour changes to the adult form. This seems to demonstrate a phase in the evolution of certain Anomuran crabs which retain many other characteristics of hermit crabs.

Another example of new information was the identification, in 1975, of a damaged decapod crustacean collected from the South China Sea by the U.S. Fisheries Steamer *Albatross* in 1908. The specimen belongs to the family Glypheidae which was known only from fossil forms appearing in the Lower Triassic and disappearing before the end of the Eocene, some 50 million years ago. In March, 1976, a French oceanographic expedition collected nine living specimens from the same locality. The species, *Neoglyphea inopinata* Forest and de Saint Laurent (1981), resembles some recent decapoda in a number of characters but also has unique features found only in fossils. The stance, the eyes and the first pereiopods, which are not chelate, make the animal look much like a praying mantis. *N. inopinata* appears to be another "living fossil" along with the fish *Latimeria chabimnae* Smith and the mollusc *Neopilina galatheae* Lemche.

TERMS USED AND ILLUSTRATED

Terms Indicated By Numbers on Figures 2–4

(The numbers in parenthesis after each term refer to the figure, or figures, on which the term is illustrated.)

1. Carapace (2a, 3b)
2. Hepatic region (2a)
3. Gastric region (2a)
4. Cardiac region (2a)
5. Branchial region (2a)
6. Intestinal region (2a)
7. Abdomen (2b, 3a, 3b)
8. Antennule with flagella (2a, 3a, 3b)
9. Antenna with flagellum (2a, 3a, 3b)
10. Eye (2a, 3a, 3b)
11. Dactylus, dactyl, or finger of cheliped (2a, 2b, 3a, 3b)
12. Thumb or fixed finger of cheliped (2a, 2b, 3a, 3b)
13. Propodus, and/or palm, of cheliped (2a, 2b, 3a, 3b)
14. Carpus (2a, 3a, 3b)
15. Merus (2a, 3a, 3b)
16. Ischium (2a, 3a, 3b)
17. Basis (2a)
18. Coxa (2a)
19. Epistome (2b)
20. Third, or outer, maxilliped (2b, 3b)
21. Mouth parts (2b)
22. Buccal cavity (2b)
23. Pterygostomian (2b)
24. Regenerating cheliped (2b)
25. Sternum (2b)
26. Telson (2b, 3a, 3b, 4)
27. First walking leg (2nd pereiopod) (2a, 2b, 3a, 3b)
28. Second walking leg (3rd pereiopod) (2a, 2b, 3a, 3b)
29. Third walking leg (4th pereiopod) (2a, 2b, 3a, 3b)
30. Fourth walking leg (5th pereiopod) (2a, 2b, 3a, 3b)
31. Shield, or hard anterior part of the carapace of a hermit crab (3a)
32. Soft, posterior part of the carapace of a hermit crab (3a)
33. Uropod (3a, 3b)

34. Pleopod (3a, 3b, 4)
35. Pleuron (3b)
36. Tergum (3b)
37. Rostrum (3a)
38. Elongate eyestalk (4)
39. Short eyestalk, cornea dilated (4)
40. Short eyestalk, cornea ovate (lateral view) (4)
41. Short eyestalk, cornea ovate (dorsal view) (4)
42. Eyescale with raised margins (4)
43. Eyescale with multispined margin (4)
44. Eyestalk of *Callianassa* with cornea not terminal (4)
45. Third maxilliped of hermit crab (4)
46. Accessory tooth on inner part of ischium (4)
47. *Crista dentata* on inner margin of ischium (4)
48. Third maxilliped of *Callianassa:* operculiform (4)
49. Third maxilliped of *Upogebia:* pediform (4)
50. Tail fan (4)
51. Sixth segment of abdomen (4)
52. Exopodite of uropod or pleopod (4)
53. Endopodite of uropod or pleopod (4)
54. Fourth walking leg (5th pereiopod) of crablike Anomura (4)
55. *Appendix interna* of 2nd pleopod of male (4)
56. *Appendix masculina* of 2nd pleopod of male (4)

Alphabetical List of Terms in Text and Illustrated by Numbers in Figures 2–4

Term	Number	Figure(s)
Abdomen	7	2b, 3a, 3b
Abdomen, 6th segment of	51	4
Accessory tooth	46	4
Antenna with flagellum	9	2a, 3a, 3b
Antennule with flagella	8	2a, 3a, 3b
Appendix interna	55	4
Appendix masculina	56	4
Basis	17	2a
Branchial region	5	2a
Buccal cavity	22	2b

15

Term	Number	Figure(s)
Carapace	1	2a, 3b
Cardiac region	4	2a
Carpus	14	2a, 3a, 3b
Coxa	18	2a
Crista dentata on ischium of 3rd maxilliped	47	4
Dactyl, dactylus, or finger of cheliped	11	2a, 2b, 3a, 3b
Endopodite	53	4
Epistome	19	2b
Exopodite	52	4
Eye	10	2a, 3a, 3b
Eyescale with raised margins	42	4
Eyescale with multispined margin	43	4
Eyestalk with cornea	38–44	4
Gastric region	3	2a
Hepatic region	2	2a
Intestinal region	6	2a
Ischium	16	2a, 3a, 3b
Merus	15	2a, 3a, 3b
Mouth parts	21	2b
Pleopod	34	3a, 3b, 4
Pleuron	35	3b
Propodus and/or palm of cheliped	13	2a, 2b, 3a, 3b
Pterygostomian	23	2b
Regenerating cheliped	24	2b
Rostrum	37	3a
Shield: anterior part of carapace of hermit crab	31	3a
Soft posterior part of the carapace of a hermit crab	32	3a
Sternum	25	2b
Tail fan	50	4
Telson	26	2b, 3a, 3b, 4
Tergum	36	3b
Third, or outer, maxilliped	20	2b, 3b
Third maxilliped of a hermit crab	45	4
Third maxilliped of *Callianassa:* operculiform	48	4

Term	Number	Figure(s)
Third maxilliped of *Upogeba:* pediform	49	4
Thumb or index finger of cheliped	12	2a, 2b, 3a, 3b
Uropod	33	3a, 3b
Walking leg, first (2nd pereiopod)	27	2a, 2b, 3a, 3b
Walking leg, second (3rd pereiopod)	28	2a, 2b, 3a, 3b
Walking leg, third (4th pereiopod)	29	2a, 2b, 3a, 3b
Walking leg, fourth (5th pereiopod)	30	2a, 2b, 3a, 3b
Walking leg (fourth) of crab-like Anomura	54	4

SEXUAL DIMORPHISM

The sex of decapod Crustacea may be ascertained by various characteristics. That of a berried female is self-evident. The most consistent character is the location of the gonopores. These small openings are usually situated on the ventral part of the coxae of the 3rd pereiopods (2nd walking legs) in the female and on the coxae of the 5th pereiopods (4th walking legs) in the male. Some female hermit crabs have only one gonopore . . . the left. Hermaphroditic species have gonopores on both areas.

In some species sexual dimorphism is a striking feature. Colour differences are not usually important, but structure of the mature male may be distinctly different from the immature male or female.

Enlarged chelipeds are found on mature males in the ghost shrimps (*Callianassa*), some *Pagurus,* all spider crabs, some pea crabs (*Pinnixa*), black-clawed crabs (*Lophopanopeus*) and shore crabs (*Hemigrapsus*). The males of the latter also have a dense pubescent patch on the inner part of the hand.

The shape of the carapace is different in the sexes of *Cryptolithodes.* The abdomen varies in width in all species in which the abdomen is bent under the thorax to form a brood pouch for the embryonic development of the eggs. Thus the width of the abdomen of a mature female is appreciably greater than that of an immature female or of a male. The exceptions to this in the Reptantia are the Families Axiidae, Callianassidae, Upogebiidae and Superfamily Paguridea.

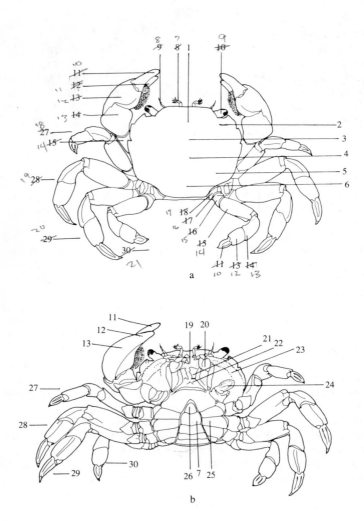

Fig. 2 Male crab: a, dorsal view; b, ventral view (For index to numbers see p. 14).

18

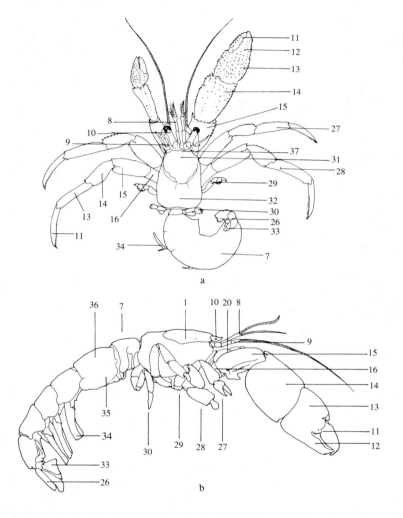

Fig. 3 Hermit crab and ghost crab: a, dorsal view (hermit crab); b, lateral view (ghost crab) (For index to numbers, see p. 14).

19

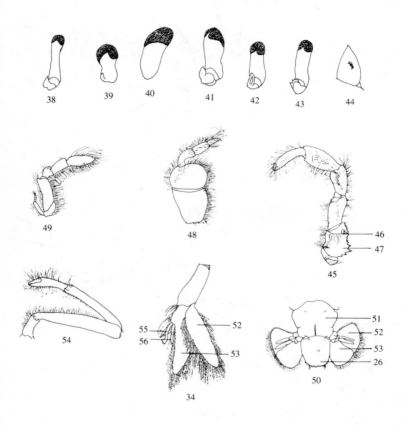

Fig. 4   Types of appendages (magnified) (For index to numbers, see p 14).

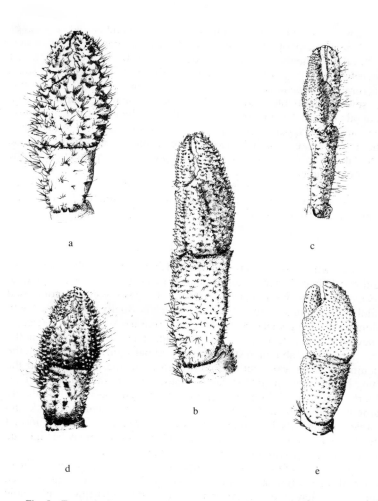

Fig. 5   Types of spines and granules on chelipeds of hermit crabs: a, large, corneous-tipped spines, tufts or stiff bristles (*Pagurus kennerlyi*); b, small, sharp spines and granules, few setae (*P. stevensae*); c, ridge with single and double row of spines (*P. stevensae*); d, intermediate size spines, long, soft setae (*P. capillatus*); e, granules and minute setae (*P. samuelis*).

There are sexual differences in the structure, number and position of the pleopods. Gonopods are developed only in some males or in hermaphrodites. They are useful in the identification of some closely related species especially among the Brachyura. Shrimps (Natantia) and some Macrura have *appendices masculinae* on the pleopods of the 2nd abdominal segment. No pleopods are developed in male Lithodidae. The pleopods of females are structured for the attachment of the egg mass. They are usually paired, except in the Paguridae and the Lithodidae, where, with few exceptions, pleopods are developed only on the left side of the abdomen which serves as a brood pouch and a protection for the developing larvae.

The males of the sand or mole crab, *Emertia analoga,* are much smaller than the females and are neotenous. They cling to the female by means of an adhesive pad.

GROWTH

The growth of crustacea is spasmodic. Like other animals encased in a rigid exoskeleton, such as insects and spiders, growth is not a gradual process like those with internal skeletons. The exoskeleton is composed mainly of a substance known as chitin, which is usually impregnated with calcium salts that give it varying degrees of rigidity. When growth occurs, a new soft shell develops inside the old. The junction between the carapace and the abdomen splits and the animal squirms out through the opening, leaving a perfect skeleton, even to all the fine hairs and the lining of the stomach and the gastric teeth. The soft-shelled animal then absorbs water and is soon perceptibly larger. The new shell gradually hardens. Until this takes place, the animal is vulnerable to attack and unable to defend itself with its soft claws, or even to retreat with normal speed. The moulting process is critical and the mortality may be high due to mechanical difficulties, as well as the dangers of predation.

Regeneration of limbs is accomplished in a fascinating manner. There is a built-in fracture zone between two of the lower sections of each appendage. Here, the internal cavity is crossed by a partition with a hole for the passage of the nerves and blood vessels. The animal can cast off the limb at this point and does so in times of stress in the same general manner that a lizard will break off its tail under duress. An advantage of this system is that the attached stump has only minimum damage to nerve and blood vessels, and the regenerating limb bud is covered by the partition. During subsequent moults the regenerated limb gradually grows until it reaches normal size.

Reptant decapod crustacea vary greatly in their rate of growth and thus some apparently have a short life-cycle while others may live for many years. It is difficult to determine the age of these animals because of the problem of marking individuals which moult all markable parts. However, commercial crabs have been studied and it has been determined that a male *Cancer magister* reaches legal size, 6½ inches across the carapace, in its fourth or fifth year.

Workers in Alaska have succeeded in tagging king crabs (*Paralithodes camtschatica*) resulting in some information about growth. The rate of growth decreases with age. In the first year the juvenile crab moults nine times, in the second year, four, in the third, twice. Thereafter a maximum of one annual moult or one every two, three, or four years takes place. Both males and females are usually mature when the carapace is over 100 mm in length. At this time they are believed to be from five to seven years old. The life span is known to reach 18 years and probably reaches a maximum of 25 years. One male crab, judged to be in its seventh year, with a carapcace of 136 × 157 mm, was tagged and recaptured six years later and 20 miles away; his carapace was then 209 × 252 mm and he was 12 pounds heavier. No female crabs, nor males with carapaces less than 178 mm (7 inches), may be taken commercially.

To judge from my studies with small decapod crustacea in still aquaria, a life span of 10 to 20 years, or even more, is not unrealistic, since I have kept mature individuals for up to 10 years.

REPRODUCTION

The sexes are separate in most reptant decapods. The gonads lie above the other organs and under the carapace and in the anterior part of the abdomen. In the Paguridea (hermit crabs) and the Thalassinidea (ghost and mud shrimps) the gonads are entirely abdominal. In those animals in which the integument is soft, (i.e. uncalcified) the location of the ovaries in the living animal can be seen as a mass of colour, which is the egg yolk, and may be yellow, orange, red, brown, green, or black.

Fertilization is internal and usually takes place immediately after the female moults. The exception to this may be in those species which produce several batches of eggs per season. There may be a special organ, called a sperm or seminal receptacle, for the storage of sperm or spermatophores until the eggs are ripe. There is often precopulatory courtship in which the male clasps the female beneath his body and carries her until she moults. The male king crab holds the female's front legs in his claws and doesn't release her until she moults. Male hermit crabs also hold a cheliped, or the edge of the shell, of the female and bump and drag her around making an audible noise, at least when confined in an aquarium. Fertilization may be accomplished using the tube formed by the gonopods (specialized pleopods) of the male to transfer the sperm to the female. Most crabs use this method. However many other reptants have no gonopods and the sperm or spermatophores are apparently transferred by the pincers of the last pair of pereiopods. This has been observed in the king crab.

There is a cementing material associated with the egg membrane. After the fertilized eggs are laid, they become attached to setae on the pleopods by a transparent twisted membrane. The eggs look like a bunch of grapes. Their number can be so great that in some crabs the abdomen is pushed out and the egg mass is only partly hidden and protected by the abdomen of the female. When the female is carrying eggs in this manner she is called "berried" or ovigerous. There is some maternal care, such as removing foreign bodies and the aeration of the developing eggs by movements of the pleopods. The eggs may be carried in this way for up to one year before hatching, but the rate of embryonic development varies in different species. In those which carry the eggs for a long period, there may be little or no embryonic development until near hatching time when development becomes rapid. In those which carry their eggs for shorter periods, or those which have several broods per year, development starts immediately after laying.

Some deep-water ghost shrimps are hermaphroditic. This is indicated by the presence of genital openings on the coxae of both the 3rd and 5th pairs of pereiopods. In one species that has been studied, the testes develop first, store the sperm and then the ovaries ripen. Because these animals do not have pigmented eyes, and live in mud in deep water, any chance encounter of two individuals can be mutually productive. Reproduction in the common earthworm is accomplished in a similar manner.

LARVAL DEVELOPMENT

Most crabs and hermit crabs pass through at least three metamorphoses in their life—zoea, megalopa and adult. The early stages are usually minute, free-swimming, planktonic forms, known as larvae, which show so few similarities to the adults that, until relatively recently, the relationships were not suspected and the larvae were described as separate species. Now they are at least recognized as larval forms even though not identifiable as to species in many cases.

The eggs of some species hatch in the last embryonic stage, the prezoea. This stage is usually brief and may result in a moult to the first larval stage almost simultaneously with hatching from the egg. The prezoea can swim by rapid movements of the abdomen, looking and acting much like the pupae of mosquitoes. The spines and setae are still invaginated and the whole animal is encased in a thin transparent film margined with delicate projections and hairs.

The first true larval stage, or zoea (Figure 6), can move through the water, usually swimming by moving the plumose setae on the well-developed maxillipeds and/or by flexing the abdomen. A brachyuran zoea is typically a minute, gnome-like creature with large black eyes, a helmet-shaped carapace with sharp spines and a tube-like, segmented abdomen terminating in a pair of sharp points. Most Anomuran zoeae are somewhat shrimp-like but there are also some bizarre forms like those of the Porcellanid, or flat-topped, crabs which have enormously elongated spines, fore and aft, and the body suspended between.

Zoeae are usually transparent and coloured only with a few branching chromatophores and with some of the exoskeleton faintly tinged. The eyes are large, with black cornea and stalked in all stages except the first. The appendages consist of a pair each of antennules, antennae, mandibles, maxillules, maxillae and from one to three pairs of functional (as swimming organs) maxillipeds. In many, two pairs of maxillipeds are equipped with four swimming setae each. The third pair, as well as the five pairs of pereiopods and the pleopods, develop slowly as the zoea moults and grows but they are not functional until the metamorphosis to the megalopa. The uropods, however, do develop and function in later zoeae of many Anomuran species but none of the Brachyurans of B.C.

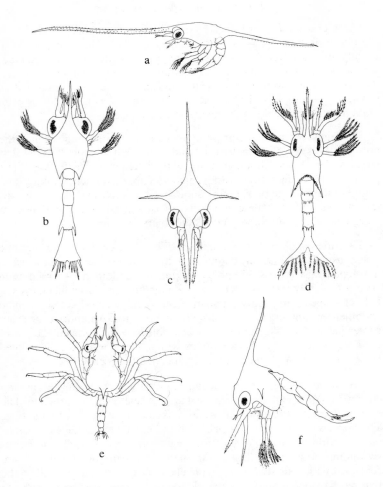

Fig. 6   Larval stages: a, zoea, flat-topped crab (*Petrolisthes*), lateral view; b, zoea, hermit crab (*Pagurus*), dorsal view; c, zoea, spider crab (*Oregonia*), anterior view; d, zoea, squat lobster (*Munida*), dorsal view; e, megalopa, spider crab (*Oregonia*), dorsal view; f, zoea, spider crab (*Oregonia*), lateral view.

Zoeae feed on smaller forms of plankton and moult at least once, but usually more often, depending on the species. The second zoea stage has stalked eyes, and six setae on the maxillipeds. At this stage development of the remainder of the appendages may be observed. The degree of development depends on the number of zoeal stages to be passed through before the final metamorphosis to the megalopal stage. In other words, if the second zoea stage is the last, the necessary growth of all appendages must be completed at this stage. But if the second zoea is one of a series of five stages it will show little indication of this growth which will not be complete until the last zoea. The pereiopods and pleopods are not functional until metamorphosis into the megalopa, which is much like the adult but differs chiefly in the form of the abdomen, where the pleopods and uropods are developed for rapid propulsion through the water. The identification of the megalopa of hermit crabs (formerly called glaucothoe) is obvious. They differ mainly from the juvenile stage by having a clearly segmented, straight abdomen and paired pleopods. The ability to swim is usually lost when the megalopa moults to produce the first juvenile stage. With subsequent growth, adult characters are gradually assumed.

Hart (1971) provides a key to planktonic larvae of families of decapod crustacea of British Columbia.

COLOUR

The colours of reptant decapod crustacea are produced by pigment granules and are composed of chemical compounds capable of selectively absorbing and reflecting certain wave lengths of light and thus producing the colours of the spectrum. In addition to the pigmentation of the calcareous impregnated integument, pigments may be contained in branched or dendritic chromatophores which can contract and expand to change colour intensity, or to mix colours. These chromatophores account for most of the colour of the larval stages of decapods but also occur in parts of the adults in which the chitinous exoskeleton is transparent or translucent. The soft parts of the carapace and the abdomen of hermit crabs fall into this category.

There are also iridescent colours which are structural and depend on physical reflection and adsorption of the light and so vary with the angle from which they are viewed. These are produced in a way similar to the rainbow colours produced by a thin film of oil on water. The iridescent colours on the integument are produced by the minute platelets in the chitin which act as a screen and produce interference colours.

ECOLOGY

Relatively little is known of the life history and ecology of crabs and hermit crabs, even for those species which are economically important. This is due to several factors: firstly, because growth is accomplished by a complete moult making marking or tagging of individuals difficult; secondly, crabs are difficult to keep in aquaria for the prolonged periods required to study their complete life history.

Crabs are usually considered to be scavengers and eaters of decayed material, but this may be a misconception for the majority of species. The large *Cancer* crabs are attracted to fish entrails or clam flesh as used in traps, but normally would seem to be predators of a variety of molluscs and other invertebrates. The king crab (*Paralithodes camschatica*) is reported from Japan to feed on mollusca, sea cucumbers, sea urchins, bryozoa and eel-grass. The gut of a large box crab (*Lopholithodes mandtii*), taken off the breakwater in Victoria, was packed with pieces of the tests and spines of sea urchins. Turtle crabs (*Cryptolithodes* sp.) feed on calcareous algae, as well as small invertebrates. Spider crabs are thought to feed on seaweed, and possibly some do, but others inhabit areas out of seaweed zones. These species are probably predators. I have kept various species in aquaria and found them to be predators under these circumstances. Many Macrura and Anomura have maxillipeds margined with dense fringes of setae, which serve as sieves to remove particles of food and plankton suspended in sea water or from detritus, which are then eaten. Until recently, pea crabs were considered to be commensals (messmates) within the bodies of molluscs and ascidians, or in the tubes of worms, but there is growing evidence that many of these should be considered as parasites. They not only remove food from their hosts but also damage the gills and other tissue of their hosts by their activities.

So-called swimming crabs of the Family Portunidae, are found in many tropical areas, such as off California and the eastern United States, where the capture of blue crabs, *Callinectes sapidus,* is an important fishery. These crabs swim by using the broadened and flattened dactyls on the last pair of legs like oars. Here, however, another type of swimming crab, the pea crab, is found. These are so small they are seldom seen. The males and, at certain phases of their development, the females, of some pea crabs develop long plumose setae on parts of their legs. The rapid vibration of these appendages enable the crabs to swim and to move from one host to another. The oceanic crabs, relatives of the common shore crabs, which can be found clinging to floating objects like glass fishing floats, swim in the same manner.

Reptant decapod crustacea occur in the waters off British Columbia from the high-water mark to as great a depth as has been investigated. They are found in all types of bottom: rocky, muddy, or sandy and are free-living or dwelling within the bodies of ascidians, clams or mussels. Some may dig their own burrows, or expropriate the empty shells of gastropod molluscs, elephant tusk shells (*Dentalium*), serpulid worm tubes, and sponges.

Study of the king crab, has resulted in the discovery of some extraordinary behaviour in one- to two-year-old juvenile crabs. These individuals congregate to form 'pods' in which each crab faces outwards and in which only those on the bottom are able to feed. The young crabs climb upon one another until they make a large ball-shaped aggregation. Such pods may join others until the mass may be as much as 12 feet long and consist of thousands of individuals. These pods occur in relatively shallow water and move slowly across the bottom. The behaviour is believed to provide protection against predation similar to that of schools in young fishes.

COMMENSALISM

Commensalism is defined as a close association between two species whereby one derives an advantage and the other usually neither advantage nor disadvantage.

The burrows made by mud shrimps, *Upogebia pugettensis* and ghost shrimps, *Callianassa californiensis*, are invaded by a number of other animals, which apparently profit from the shelter and probably share the food of the hosts. These include two species of copepod crustacea, *Hemicyclops thysanotus* and *H. subadhaerens*, which live on the surfaces of the hosts but are capable of swimming freely. Other crustacea which may be present are a hooded shrimp, *Betaeus harrimani*, and the pea crabs, *Pinnixa schmitti* and *Scleroplax granulata*. A polychaete scale worm, *Hesperonoe complanata*, and a fish, the arrow goby, *Clevelandia ios*, may also occur. A bivalved mollusc, *Orobitella* (formerly *Pseudopythina*) *rugifera*, lives attached by byssus threads to the pleopods of *Upogebia pugettensis*.

Several of the larger hermit crabs have a commensal polychaete worm, *Cheilonereis cyclurus*, occupying the same shell. *C. cyclurus* is a large, brown and white worm which appears at meal time to catch the "crumbs". Another polychaete worm, *Polydora commensalis*, either burrows into the gastropod shell or creates a tube for itself by bridging the columella groove in the central pillar with a calcareous film. This animal is particulary common in the shells occupied by *Pagurus granosimanus*.

There is an extraordinary symbiotic or parasitic association between some lithodid crabs and certain liparid fish. In California and in British Columbia *Lopholithodes foraminatus* has been found to harbour, in the gill cavity, the developing eggs of the black-tail liparid or snail fish, *Careproctus melanurus*. *Paralithodes camtschatica* is also such a host, but apparently to a different species of fish because *C. melanurus* is not found within the range of this crab (Peden and Corbett 1973).

An interesting form of commensalism may be seen on shells occupied by certain hermit crabs. A hydroid called *Hydractinia*, settles on the margin of the shell and develops a firm base which extends outwards as the colony grows. This so enlarges the shell that it is not necessary for the hermit crab to search for a larger shell after growth by moulting. Thus the hydroid continues to benefit from the association and transportation for a longer period of time than would be possible otherwise.

There are commensal sea anemones, some of which live on the shells occupied by hermit crabs. Here, I have seen them only on deep-sea species, *Parapagurus pilosimanus benedicti* and *Pagurus tanneri*. In European waters a sea anemone, *Calliactis parasitica*, lives on a whelk shell, *Buccinum undatum*, when it is inhabited by a hermit crab. This anemone can transfer itself from one shell to another by clinging with its tentacles and releasing and moving the pedal disc (base). In some cases this behaviour is helped by the host. Apparently in this association the hermit crab gains a protective cover because it has been determined that an octopus is repelled by the presence of the anemone. The transportation provided is beneficial to the anemone.

A sponge, *Suberites ficus,* settles on a gastropod shell occupied by a hermit crab and grows in all directions, surrounding the hermit crab, but leaving a spiral space so that the animal can still navigate. The sponge becomes quite large and somewhat boat-shaped. The presence of the sponge dissolves the calcium carbonate of the original shell so that only the soft organic parts of the shell remain.

PARASITES

Decapod crustacea are hosts to a number of external parasites. These may appear as abnormal growths, usually on the abdomen, or the branchial area may be greatly swollen on one side. The deformities are caused by species of other orders of crustacea: barnacles (Cirripedia) and wood-lice or pill bugs (Isopoda).

The parasitic barnacles (Rhizocephala) are greatly modified and quite unrecognizable as adult barnacles but the free-swimming larval stages are typical barnacle larvae. The final larval stage finds the right host, metamorphoses, casting off eyes and appendages. The remaining tissues then enter the body of the host and penetrate the digestive tract with nutritive rootlets, as well as invading most of the internal organs. When the parasite matures, a portion erupts through the abdominal wall and appears as a soft, sac-like growth, attached by a peduncle. This sac contains male and female reproductive organs as well as a brood pouch. These growths may be globose, sausage- or boat-shaped. The parasite usually castrates its host.

These parasites may be host-specific or they may occur on several allied species. In British Columbia relatively few species of decapod crustacea are attacked and the percentage of individuals within these species so affected is small. One species of true crabs, four of lithodid crabs and about a dozen species of hermit crabs have been found to be infested occasionally.

Species of isopod (Family Bopyridae) parasitize some members of the Macrura and Anomura. They are usually found in the branchial cavity of the host, but one species, *Phyllodurus abdominalis,* (Figure 7) occurs under the abdomen of the mud shrimp, *Upogebia pugettensis.* These isopods are only slightly modified because of their parasitic life. The female is obese, with short prehensile feet and a ventral brood pouch. The male is small, slender, and normally found clinging to the body of the

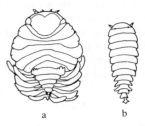

Fig. 7   The isopod parasite *Phyllodurus abdominalis*: a, female, dorsal view; b, male, dorsal view.

female. The host often suffers damage to the gills, due to the presence of the parasite as well as a severe swelling of the carapace in the branchial region. Only mud shrimps and ghost shrimps, a few species of hermit crabs, and squat lobsters are known to be infested in the waters off British Columbia.

Hermit crabs are infested by a number of species of Rhizocephala. Those that have been recorded here are: *Argulosaccus tenuis*, *Clistosaccus paguri*, *Peltogaster boschmae*, *P. paguri*, *Peltogasterella gracilis* and *Thompsonia* spp. Lithodid crabs *Lithodes aequispinus*, *L. couesi* and *Paralithodes camtschatica* have *Briarosaccus callosus* and *Hapalogaster mertensii*, *Briarosaccus tennellus*. The black-clawed crab, *Lophopanopeus bellus* is host to *Loxothylacus panopaei*.

Parasitic isopods here: *Ione cornuta* on the ghost shrimp, *Callianassa californiensis*; hermit crabs have *Pseudione giardi* and squat lobsters *Pseudione galancantae* and *Munidion parvum*. In California *Pachycheles rudis* is parasitized by *Aporobopyrus muguensis* and *P. pubescens* by *A. oviformis*. These may be here also, but have not yet been recorded.

COLLECTING

More than half of the known reptant decapods of British Columbia occur in the intertidal or high, subtidal area. This means that collecting can be done at low tide or in shallow water by SCUBA or snorkel, or with small, hand-operated dredges. Animals of deep-water habitat are usually obtained by dredging or trapping. In abyssal areas this becomes a slow and expensive process. Even material from the continental shelf is not easily come by, particularly in the Pacific Ocean. New distribution records and new species are still being found. In the last 25 years the number of species recorded from British Columbia waters has increased by 50 per cent, due perhaps to more scientific collection and to research on the material so obtained.

Crabs may be preserved by placing in a 5–10% solution of formalin (formaldehyde) and water . . . preferably sea water. This mixture seems to preserve the colour much longer than when fresh water is used. After several days the specimens can be dried and mounted if desired. Unfortunately the colours do not keep well when dried and the specimens are fragile. Small crabs, or their moulted skins, can be embedded in plastic quite satisfactorily. Isopropyl alcohol, at 40%, or 70% ethanol are also used and make a more permanent preservation than 5–10% formalin. But, in these preparations, the colour fades almost immediately. If living specimens are placed in any of these fluids, there is a tendency for the animal to cast off legs. The most satisfactory way to prevent this is to slowly raise the temperature of the sea water in a container to about 50°C (120°F). At this temperature, the animal relaxes and dies without self-mutilation.

ECONOMIC IMPORTANCE

Only one species of crab is fished commercially in British Columbia. This is *Cancer magister,* the commercial, Dungeness, or Pacific, crab. The main crab fisheries are around the Queen Charlotte Islands, Hecate Strait and Dixon Entrance, off the west coast of Vancouver Island, and in Boundary Bay and Burrard Inlet. Crab traps are used but many crabs are obtained, incidentally, by trawlers fishing for groundfish.

In other areas, the catch of Japanese or Alaska king crab, is an important fishery. This species does occur in northern British Columbia but, because we are at the southern limit of its range, the numbers caught are not great. *Chionoecetes bairdi,* found at less than 500 m depth, *C. tanneri* found only deeper than 500 m and *C. angulatus,* found only deeper than 1500 m, may in time be used commercially. *C. opilio* from waters off eastern Canada, Alaska and Japan, is now sold canned as "Canadian crab meat" or "Atlantic Queen Crab" and, frozen, as "Alaska snow crab" and/or "Japanese or Korean snow crab". How feasible a commercial fishery of the British Columbia species of these spider crabs would be, is not known at this time.

33

Non-commercial utilization of edible crustacea is controlled by regulations of the government of Canada. A free pamphlet containing information about these regulations, and entitled *British Columbia Tidal Waters Sport Fishing Guide,* is issued annually. It can be obtained from Marine Resources Branch, Ministry of Environment, Parliament Buildings, Victoria, B.C. V8V 1X4. Only male crabs may be taken. *Cancer magister* must be at least 6½ inches (16.5 cm) and *C. productus* 4½ inches (11.5 cm) across the carapace. The allowable daily catch varies in different parts of the Province.

Reptant decapoda crustacea are of economic importance for reasons other than human consumption. The free-swimming larvae form an important component of plankton, particularly during spring and summer. They are consumed by various predators and thus form links in the food chain, especially in inshore waters. *Cancer gacilis* is a predator and may eat large numbers of small oyster spat; therfore, these depredations can be of considerable importance to the oyster farmer. Two species of Anomura, *Munida* sp. and *Acantholithodes hispidus,* eat shrimp and will enter shrimp traps and feed on the captives, thus decreasing the catch for the fisherman.

CLASSIFICATION

Plants and animals are classified by scientists into a system of groups or divisions. The basic unit of this system is the species. A species may be defined as a group of individuals able to breed successfully with one another but not with individuals of another group.

The constructions and terminology of this system is as follows:

Species
Genus
Subfamily
Family
Superfamily
Subsection
Section
Suborder
Order
Class
Phylum

How this system applies to the reptant decapod crustacea can be seen in the Checklist of Species Treated in This Book (pp. 38–42).

The scientific names of the animals in the divisions in this system are Latin, or Latinized words from other languages, and, since there are always at least two words in each name, the system is known as the Binomial System of Nomenclature. The first word in the name refers to the genus to which the species belongs; the second serves to identify the species itself. A third word may appear in a name; then the animal referred to is a subspecies.

For example, the name *Parapagurus pilosimanus benedicti* refers to a hermit crab of the genus *Parapagurus*, the species *pilosimanus*, and the subspecies *benedicti*.

By convention, scientific names are printed in italic type. The names and dates, which sometimes follow scientific names, refer to the authority who originally described the species and to the date that description was published. These are printed in Roman type. When the author and date are enclosed in parentheses it means that changes in the original classification of the species have subsequently taken place.

In this book, where available, common or vernacular names are also given. But, since these can vary from place to place, and in time, to avoid possible confusion, readers should get to know scientific names. These have world-wide acceptance and change only when sound scientific support for such a change is found.

Decapod crustacea are divided into two Suborders; the swimmers, or Natantia, which includes all true shrimps, and the crawlers, or Reptantia. Only the latter are dealt with in this book.

The Reptantia are divided into three Sections:

1. The Macrura, shrimp-like or lobster-like animals with large, straight, symmetrical abdomens, well-developed pleopods and a tail fan.
2. The Anomura, include hermit crabs and crab-like Anomura as well as other crabs with symmetrical abdomens, such as squat lobsters, porcelain crabs and sand crabs. In all, the last pair of walking legs is small and not used for walking. Usually these serve as cleaners and, when not in use, are folded and hidden beneath the carapace.
3. The Brachyura, which include the true crabs with small, flattened, symmetrical abdomens which are bent under the body. They have no uropods and the walking legs are alike and used for locomotion only.

35

HOW TO USE THIS BOOK

To help identify the various crabs and allied species in this book, a series of keys is presented. Each is made up of a number of pairs of statements which serve to place the animals concerned into smaller groups separated by more detailed differences.

The process of identifying a specimen begins with determining the Section to which it belongs. Next find the Family and from that key, the genus and species. Once that has been done, check your identification with the description of the species. If these agree, then you can be reasonably sure that you are right. If they do not agree, then you probably have made a mistake in interpretation. If so, try again.

For example, if your specimen is crab-like, with a symmetrical abdomen bent under the body and has four pairs of similar walking legs, Section Brachyura would be the choice. If the mouth parts are somewhat square in outline, the rostrum large, pointed and divided into two parts, and the eyes not enclosed in orbits, Subsection Oxyrhyncha is indicated and the Family Majidae. Then, if the body and appendages are hairy, walking legs long and slender, rostrum of two long horns, slim and parallel, the specimen should be the spider crab *Oregonia gracilis*. Check the description and illustrations of this species for confirmation and additional information.

Large, adult, male crabs may be quite different in shape and proportions to immature males and females. Thus I have tried to use distinguishing characters which are stable during the life of the individual. Faded, superficially alike, hermit crabs can be difficult to identify. An examination of the telson may often confirm or reject a questionable species, therefore each species illustrated includes a magnified sketch of the telson.

Because of individual variation, the illustration may not always look like the specimen at hand, but if it conforms to the description, the identification is probably correct.

In this book, I have attempted to keep the descriptions brief and to emphasize differences between closely allied and often similar species. If a more detailed description is desired, consult the References. When more than one species of a genus is described, brief notes on the characteristics of the genus are given. Since these apply to all species of the genus, they are not repeated in the descriptions. In some cases the characters used to separate allied species may be too small to be determined by the naked eye. Therefore, some type of magnification is required. Small hermit crabs and pea crabs are in this category.

The various types of projections of the surface of crabs are of value in the identification of species. Unfortunately the terminology of these cannot be clearly defined because descriptions by various authors use different criteria. Granules, tubercules and knobs may all apply to the same protruding parts. Teeth, serrated margins and spines can also be interchangeable and yet vary greatly. These may have sharp points, are sometimes corneous and, except for hinged or movable spines, all are rigid projections. They may also be flat-topped, long and narrow, short and wide, spined and/or setose. Setae also occur in a great variety of forms and have many different, known and unknown, functions. Long, thin, soft setae may be termed 'hair'; dense patches of fine short setae 'pubescence'; long, flexible feather-like setae with numerous fine filaments are 'plumose' and may be used for swimming (natatory) or serve as nets to sieve detritus or to catch plankton. Bristles are stiff setae which may be modified to form a type of barbless hook to which spider crabs attach various materials thus providing a camouflage. (Such crabs are often called decorator crabs.) The ends of the last two pairs of walking legs, and the uropods, of hermit crabs have rows of stout, short, corneous setae which form rasps and serve as grasping organs to prevent the animal from being pulled from its protective shell. Many of the lithodid crabs have specialized setae which are enclosed in minute club, or capitate, balloon-like films.

Colour notes have rarely been reported in the literature; therefore, during my years of study of the decapod crustacea of British Columbia, I have kept detailed notes and coloured drawings of the living animals. In the following descriptions an attempt has been made to describe the usual colouration found and to give a range of variations which occur in some species. These colour patterns can be quite specific, especially in the hermit crabs and the pea crabs, and are useful in identification while collecting. Unfortunately, the colour changes or fades on preservation.

An insert, following page 60, provides coloured illustrations of 25 of the species treated in this work. The species illustrated represent only a sample of the variety and extent of colour in these animals. Species so illustrated are indicated by an * beside their scientific name in the text treating them.

Habitat, largest known size, and depth records are taken from the literature, except where my unpublished data gives new information. For each species, the scientific name currently used is given first, in bold-face type, with the author and date of publication. Below these are the scientific names formerly used. Common names, if applicable, are to the right of the scientific names.

There are a number of species which occur in the northeastern Pacific Ocean which apparently have not yet been described. Until more research is done and revisions are made, incorrect identification of some specimens is almost unavoidable. Any decapod crustacea collected from depths greater than 366m (200 fathoms) should be carefully examined because it may be a rarely found species, a new record for the area, or even an undescribed form. Forty years ago, 69 species of reptant decapod crustacea had been recorded from British Columbia (Hart 1940). Today there are more than 90.

CHECKLIST OF SPECIES TREATED IN THIS BOOK

Phylum ARTHROPODA
  Class CRUSTACEA
    Order DECAPODA
      Suborder REPTANTIA

SECTION MACRURA

Superfamily Thalassinidea

Key to Families

1. Shrimp-like. Integument soft and pleura on abdomen large. Live in burrows..Axiidae

1. Shrimp-like. Integument soft and pleura small. Live in burrows..2

2. Rostrum distinct, ridged and setose. Eyestalks cylindrical and cornea terminal. Chelipeds subchelate and subequal ....Upogebiidae

2. Rostrum minute and smooth. Eyestalks flattened with mid-dorsal corneal pigment or cylindrical without dark pigment. Chelipeds chelate and unequal in size and shape..........Callianassidae

Family AXIIDAE

The thin-shelled shrimp-like animals in this family are all burrowers and are found from shallow subtidal habitats to great depths. Recently Pemberton, Risk and Buckley (1976) determined that one species found off Nova Scotia makes burrows more than 2.5 m into the substrate. Obviously in abyssal regions the collection of these animals under such circumstances is particularly haphazard. Thus the number of specimens obtained is few and often these are damaged. Four species of this family are known to occur in the waters off British Columbia. All have one or two small hollow knobs of apparently unknown function on the mid-dorsal ridge of the carapace. These species have been assigned to the genera *Axiopsis, Calastacus* and *Calocaris*. The definitions of these genera were made when few species had been studied and recent discoveries indicate that the criteria used are not satisfactory. New genera will have to be created and the taxonomy of the Family revised. It is important that any specimens obtained should be carefully preserved and placed in suitable research collections where they will be available for future study.

Family Axiidae

Key to Species

1. Eyes with dark pigment. Known from less than 200 m depth
....*Axiopsis spinulicauda*
1. Eyes without pigment. Known only from more than 200 m
depth 2
2. Rostrum slender with 2 teeth at base and no spines on dorsal
carapace or telson ....*Calastacus stilirostris*
2. Rostrum flat and wide with lateral teeth. Spines on ridges of
carapace and on telson...3
3. 2 ridges with spines on carapace. Numerous small granules
on carapace and some parts of appendages *Calocaris investigatoris*
3. 5 ridges with spines on carapace; carapace surface smooth.
Small spines on hands of chelipeds............*Calocaris quinqueseriatus*

Axiopsis spinulicauda (Rathbun 1902)*
Axius spinulicauda

Description—Carapace surface smooth. Large, flattened, rostrum with toothed margins extends as a sharp ridge on either side of gastric area. A toothed ridge runs medially nearly to cervical groove. Between these 3 ridges are 2 shorter ones. A raised area protrudes in the centre of the posterior margin. Eyestalk stout with pigmented cornea. Antenna with long projections or "thorns" on second and third basal segments. Chelipeds unequal in size; palm of large cheliped of male subrectangular with margins cut into numerous teeth, as is the dactyl. Palm of large cheliped of female with slightly curved margins and long slender fingers. Small chelipeds with finely toothed, curved margins and smaller teeth. Walking legs slender, setose and subequal in length, and first one chelate. Abdomen smooth, stout and pleura broad with rounded margins. Taii fan with telson and distal margin strongly curved and longer than 6th segment and uropods. Telson with a tooth on mid-posterior margin. Rows of spines on distal surface of telson and on mid-ridges of uropods. Outer margins of uropods toothed. Paired pleopods on abdominal segments 1–5; uniramous on 1st and rest biramous and foliacious with *appendix interna*. Male with *appendix masculina* as well on 2nd pleopod. Eggs are carried on all pleopods of the female.

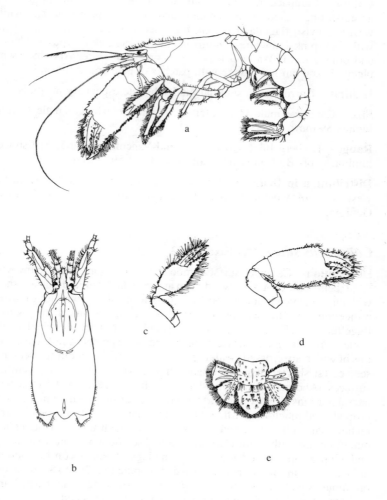

Fig. 8   *Axiopsis spinulicauda*: a, male, lateral view; b, male carapace, dorsal view; c, male, right cheliped; d, female, right cheliped; e, male, tail fan.

Colour—Carapace translucent pink with coral rostrum and ridges with greenish tinge laterally. Antennules and antennae pale pink and white with yellowish flagella. Eyestalk translucent, cornea black. Chelipeds with shell-pink and white ischium and merus, coral red carpus and hand, and orange teeth. Walking legs pink, coral and white. Abdomen with pleopods and tail fan orange with patches of pale orange or pink.

Habitat—Burrowers in subtidal mud substrate especially in fjords.

Size—Carapace: male 33 mm, female 30 mm. Total length: male 90 mm, female 89 mm.

Range—Holberg Inlet, Quatsino Sound Vancouver Island, British Columbia, to off Bodega Head, California; from 59–256 m.

Distribution in British Columbia—Recorded from the fjords on the west coast of Vancouver Island and from Stuart Channel, Strait of Georgia.

Calastacus stilirostris Faxon 1893

Description—Carapace surface smooth. Rostrum long and narrow with stout teeth at base. A narrow ridge on anterior dorsal area. Eyestalk short with unpigmented globular cornea. Peduncle of antenna with long narrow projections or "thorns" on 2nd and 3rd segments and a long setose flagellum. Chelipeds large, subequal and with sharp marginal teeth, some spines on inner surface of palm and no gape between fingers, the tips of which are crossed. Walking legs slender, with smooth surfaces and setose, 1st shorter than others and chelate with fine spines on cutting surfaces. Abdomen relatively slender with well developed pleura with lateral margins slightly angled. Tail fan with telson subequal in length to uropods and much longer than 6th abdominal segment. Telson elongate rectangular with 2 unarmed ridges. Uropods with unarmed ridges and outer margins with teeth. Hermaphrodites, so gonopores on coxae of 3rd and 5th pereiopods (2nd and 4th walking legs). Pleopods on 1st abdominal segment, uniramous and modified for copulation. 2nd to 5th pleopods biramous, slender and with *appendix interna* and long setae, particularly on base where bits of egg membrane may still be attached.

Colour—Unrecorded.

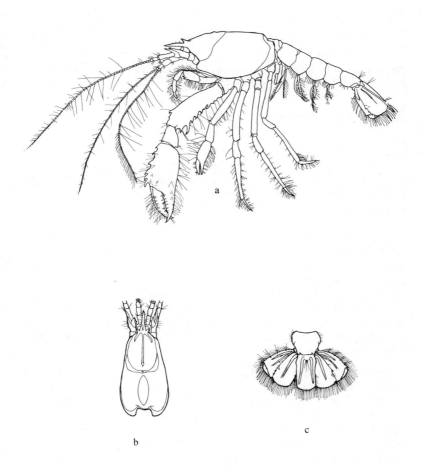

Fig. 9 *Calastacus stilirostris*: a, lateral view; b, carapace, dorsal view; c, tail fan.

47

Habitat—Brown sand or rock.

Size—Carapace 22 mm; total length 52 mm.

Range—From southwestern British Columbia to Peru (16°S, 73°27′W); 700 to 1208 m.

Distribution in British Columbia—One record: September 1964, southwest of Vancouver Island (47°58′N, 125°47.2′W); from 924 m.

Calocaris investigatoris (Anderson 1896)
Calastacus investigatoris, Calocaris (Calocaris) granulosus

Description—Carapace surface covered with fine, sharp granules. A sharp mid-dorsal ridge. Rostrum flat with teeth on margins which extend as ridges on gastric area. Cervical and branchial grooves. Eyestalk small and cornea without pigment. Antenna with short projections or "thorns" on 2nd and 3rd segments of peduncle. Chelipeds subequal, with fine marginal teeth, outer face of palm with 3 rows of granules. Fingers long and narrow with a gape proximally. Walking legs slender and setose, 1st chelate and shorter than others. Hermaphroditic so gonopores on coxae of 2nd and 4th walking legs. Abdomen long, setose with broad pleura which has grooves and knobs and lateral margins rounded. Tail fan with telson longer than uropods and twice as long as 6th abdominal segment. Two rows of fine spines converging proximally. Uropods with a few teeth on outer margins. Pleopods on 1st segment small and uniramous, modified for copulation. Pleopods on segments 2 to 5 biramous, slender, setose and with *appendix interna* only.

Colour—Carapace pale grey with white rostrum, crest, grooves and hollow tubercle. Coral of yolk of eggs in ovary visible through translucent carapace. Chelipeds and walking legs pale orange with white teeth and pale yellow setae. Ischium and merus lighter in colour than terminal segments. Abdomen pinkish orange, deepest ventrally and pleura white. Pleopods and tail fan pale pink. Antennules and antennae pale grey dorsally and orange ventrally. Eyestalk orange, deepest distally with translucent orange cornea.

Habitat—Abyssal mud.

Size—Carapace 25 mm; total length 60 mm.

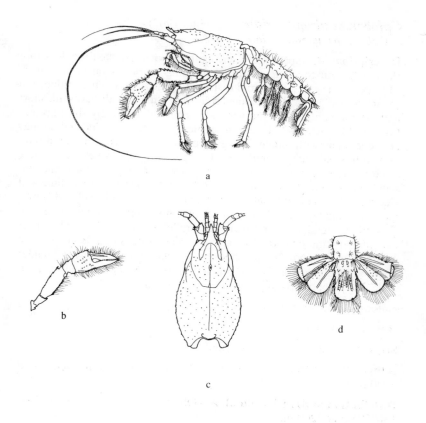

Fig. 10 *Calocaris investigatoris*: a, lateral view; b, right cheliped; c, carapace, dorsal view; d, tail fan.

Range—Arabian Sea. South of Sannak Islands, Aleutian Islands, Alaska, to San Diego, California; from 549 to 1733 m.

Distribution in British Columbia—Off Englefield Bay, Queen Charlotte Islands (53°01.5'N, 132°54.3'W); at 1069 m.

Calocaris quinqueseriatus (Rathbun 1902)
Calastacus quinqueseriatus

Description—Carapace surface smooth, cervical groove deep. Rostrum flattened, with toothed margins continuing as ridges on gastric area. Median ridge spined from mid rostrum to gastric area. These ridges are separated by 2 more short, spined ridges, making 5 in all. Eyestalk short and cornea without dark pigment. Antenna with relatively short projections or "thorns" on 2nd and 3rd segment of peduncle. Unequal, elongated chelipeds with toothed margins and surface of hands covered with numerous small sharp granules. A slight gape proximally between fingers of large cheliped but none on smaller. 1st walking leg short and chelate, with spines on posterior margin of ischium and merus. Others long and slender with setae terminally. Abdomen stout; pleura broad and lateral margins rounded. Tail fan with telson only slightly longer than 6th abdominal segment: lateral margins parallel and toothed, distal margin curved and with a median tooth. Two, spined ridges on telson and 1 on endopod of uropod. No pleopod on 1st abdominal segment. Slender biramous pleopods on 2nd to 5th segments with *appendix interna*. In male 2nd pleopod has an *appendix masculina* as well.

Colour—Unrecorded.

Habitat—Abyssal mud.

Size—Carapace 27 mm; total length 73 mm.

Range—Sea of Okhotsk, and off San Nicolas Island, California; 288 to 2200 m.

Distribution in British Columbia—Off Vancouver Island (50°54.3'N, 130°6'W); at 2200 m.

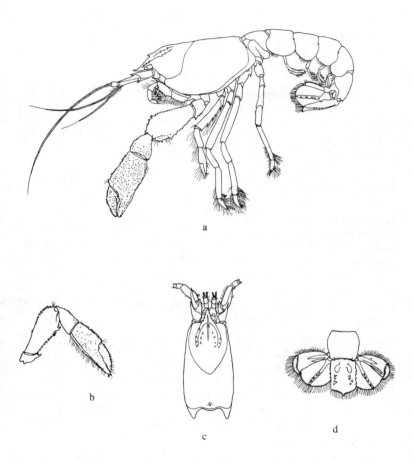

Fig. 11 *Calocaris quinqueseriatus*: a, male, lateral view; b, male, right cheliped;
c, male, carapace, dorsal view; d, tail fan.

51

Family UPOGEBIIDAE

Key to Species

1. Third maxillipeds pediform. Walking legs with simple dactyls. Littoral and subtidal ....*Upogebia pugettensis*

The Genus *Upogebia* Leach 1814

Shrimp-like. Rostrum short, tridentate and setose. Chelipeds subequal and subchelate. Last walking leg chelate, rest simple. Eyestalk cylindrical and cornea terminal. Third maxillipeds pediform. First 2 pairs of pleopods different from last 3 which are foliaceous and have *appendices internae*.

Upogebia pugettensis (Dana 1852)   Mud Shrimp
Gebia pugettensis, G. californica

Description—Carapace with anterior dorsal area rough and setose with rest smooth and membranous. Chelipeds setose, stout with small thumb and stout dactyl. Walking legs stout, slightly compressed and setose. Abdomen with narrow pleura and pubescence on 3rd, 4th and 5th segments. Male without pleopods on 1st segment. Large and foliaceous pleopods on segments 2 to 5. Female with uniramous pleopods on segment 1 and foliaceous on 2 to 5. All except the last pair serve to carry eggs. Telson wider than long.

Colour—Considerable variation in intensity and distribution of colour. Carapace with anterior part blue and brown, laterally grey or white with reticulations of blue, orange or yellow. Abdomen brown with blue and green reticulations. Tail fan with a symmetrical pattern of blue and green on sixth segment, bright yellow with blue ridges on uropods and telson orange margined with green. Pleopods orange. Chelipeds: ischium orange, merus and carpus yellow and blue with pale brown setae. Hand blue with tip of dactyl white. Eyestalk orange, cornea black.

Habitat—Common in burrows in muddy sand, but are also found in most sheltered beaches as well, in sand or gravel, particularly under rocks where sufficient suitable material is available to construct semi-permanent burrows. Y-shaped burrows with several openings on the surface are made.

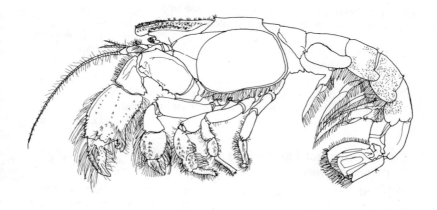

Fig. 12 *Upogebia pugettensis*: male, lateral view.

Size—Total length: male, 150 mm; female 105 mm.

Range—Valdez Narrows, Alaska (60°4′N, 146°40′W), to San Quentin Bay, Mexico; intertidal.

Distribution in British Columbia—Common in suitable habitats.

Notes—Of some economic importance due to burrowing activities. On certain types of oyster beds, young oysters can be smothered by the mud displaced by these animals. Also dykes designed to retain a layer of sea water may be riddled with burrows through which water drains at low tide.

Family CALLIANASSIDAE
Key to Species

1. Eyestalks flattened with small pigmented cornea mid-dorsal. Third maxillipeds operculiform. Littoral and subtidal 2
1. Eyestalks cylindrical and with cornea unpigmented. Third maxillipeds pediform with semicircular dactyl. Abyssal......
....*Callianopsis goniophthalma*
2. Large cheliped with sharp straight dorsal ridge on carpus. Small cheliped with carpus and merus subequal in width
....*Callianassa gigas*
2. Large cheliped with sharp dorsal ridge incurved laterally on carpus. Small cheliped with carpus wider than merus............
....*Callianassa californiensis*

Callianopsis goniophthalma (Rathbun 1901)
Callianassa goniopthalma

Description—Shrimp-like. Carapace smooth and membranous with a slight elevation on mid-dorsal margin. Rostrum small but distinct and sharp pointed. Antennules and antennae setose with long slender flagella. Eyestalk sub-oblong, with a small tooth, and cornea without dark pigment. Third maxillipeds pediform and dactyls semicircular. Chelipeds unlike and unequal in size. Larger cheliped much longer than carapace, with narrow merus with a ventral marginal tooth; carpus wide with slightly convex outer surface and hand with sharp margins and a gape between fingers of male but not of female. Small cheliped slender with subequal merus and carpus which are shorter than hand. 1st walking leg chelate, 2nd and 3rd with simple dactyls and last subchelate with a flared tip on dactyl. Abdomen more than twice as long as carapace, with narrow pleura and a sharp tooth on either side of 6th segment. Tail fan with sub-rectangular telson slightly shorter than uropods and no tooth on distal margin. 1st pair of pleopods of male are gonopods with the terminal part flat and boat-shaped, 2nd to 5th foliaceous. Female with 1st pair of pleopods biramous and slender, and 2nd to 5th foliaceous.

Colour—Unrecorded.

Habitat—Deep water, probably in burrows.

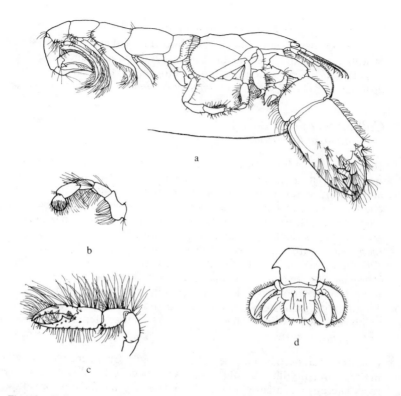

Fig. 13 *Callianopsis goniophthalma*: a, male, lateral view; b, male, third maxilliped; c, male, left cheliped; d, tail fan.

Size—Total length: male 130 mm, female 100 mm.

Range—Clarence Strait, Alaska, to off Harris Point, San Miguel Island, California; from 483 to 651 m.

Distribution in British Columbia—No known record but it undoubtedly occurs in British Columbia waters because it has been taken in Clarence Strait, northeast of Queen Charlotte Islands and from off the mouth of the Columbia River.

The Genus *Callianassa* Leach 1814

Shrimp-like. Rostrum small. Chelipeds unequal and chelate. 1st pair of walking legs small, equal and chelate, 2nd and last subchelate. Eyestalk flattened. Third maxillipeds operculiform. 1st two pairs of pleopods different from last 3 which have *appendices internae* and are foliaceous.

Callianassa gigas Dana 1852   Ghost Shrimp
Callianassa longimana

Description—Adult males are easily distinguished from *C. californiensis* males, but immature males and females of the two species are alike and require careful comparison to separate. Adult male has unlike chelipeds, one much larger than the other. The larger may be subequal in length to the entire animal. Dorsal and ventral margins of carpus and hand are relatively straight, the outer face with longitudinal groove ventrally, merus stout with large proximal ventral lobe. Large cheliped of female and immature male with hand longer than carpus, and merus with a large lobe near base. In both sexes small cheliped differs from *C. californiensis* in being proportionately more slender, with carpus and hand subequal. 1st walking leg chelate with palm wider than that of *C. californiensis*. 2nd to 4th walking legs similar but proportions slightly different. Pleopods as in *C. californiensis*.

Colour—Carapace ivory, pale yellow and pink. Chelipeds ivory. Walking legs cream with red-gold setae. Abdomen flesh-coloured dorsally, ivory laterally and areas of pink, rose and yellow. Tail fan pink or yellow, pleopods yellow.

Habitat—Burrrow in mud or sandy mud, low intertidal and subtidal.

Size—Total length: male 150 mm, female 106 mm.

Range—Tobey Point, and Dodge Cove, Digby Island, British Columbia (54°15′N, 130°20′W), to San Quentin Bay, Mexico; intertidal to 50 m.

Distribution in British Columbia—Few records, mainly off southern Vancouver Island and near Prince Rupert, probably due to difficulty of collection and identification.

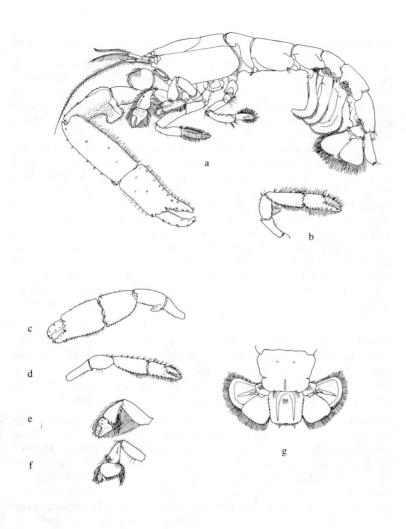

Fig. 14 *Callianassa gigas*: a, male, lateral view; b, male, right cheliped; c, female, left cheliped; d, female, right cheliped; e, female, left 2nd pereiopod; f, female, left 3rd pereiopod; g, male tail fan.

Callianassa californiensis Dana 1854   Ghost Shrimp

Description—Surface smooth and membranous. Flattened eyestalk pointed and divergent with pigmented cornea mid-dorsally. Antennules and antennae with long, somewhat setose, flagella. Chelipeds unlike and unequal, the larger may be either left or right; surface glossy and compressed, with sharp margins, thin, and slightly curved dorsally. Merus relatively slender with a prominent lobe ventrally. In adult male large cheliped with carpus and hand subequal in length and breadth, but immature male and female with hand longer than carpus. Small hand of male and female has carpus longer than hand and fingers shorter than palm. 1st walking legs flattened, setose and chelate, 2nd also setose with triangular carpus, broad subrectangular propodus and small rounded dactyl. 3rd and 4th legs slender with tufts of stiff setae on propodus and dactyl; last leg chelate. Narrow pleura with pubescence on 3rd, 4th and 5th segments. Male with vestigial pleopods on 1st abdominal segment and none on 2nd. Female with egg-carrying uniramous pleopods on 1st segment and biramous on 2nd. Pleopods 3 to 5 are foliaceaous and used for backward propulsion. Tail fan with broad flat uropods and subrectangular telson, which is slightly longer than wide and has a tooth on midposterior margin.

Colour—Clear bright colours. Carapace and chelipeds mainly white with patches of yellow, orange, flesh-pink or rose. Walking legs pale pink. Abdomen pink, deep rose and some tinges of yellow. Pleopods white or cream and tail fan often yellow. Eyestalk orange with black cornea. Adult males usually with more white areas than females.

Habitat—Live in burrows excavated in sand or sandy mud in high intertidal. In certain areas tremendous numbers may be found but these are much smaller in size than in areas where the numbers are less. High up on sandy beaches holes about 5 mm in diameter indicate the presence of these animals. Under the surface the burrow widens to about 20 mm and is smoothly plastered with mud and is usually vertical for perhaps 50 cm, then runs horizontal for some distance before rising to the surface again. It is difficult to excavate an entire burrow because the wet sand is so unstable. In highly populated areas collection is relatively simple but in areas where there are fewer and the animals larger and the burrows deeper, much and often fruitless digging is required.

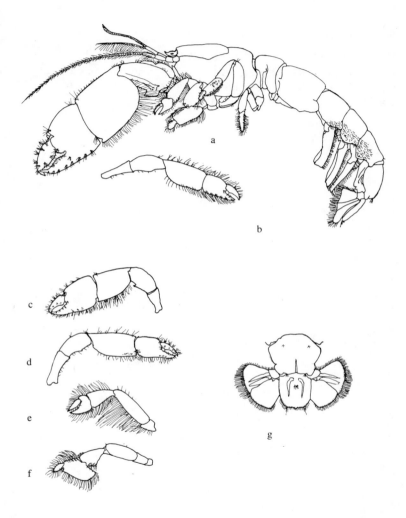

Fig. 15 *Callianassa californiensis*: a, male, lateral view; b, male, right cheliped; c, female, left cheliped; d, female, right cheliped; e, female, left 2nd pereiopod; f, female, left 3rd pereiopod; g, male, tail fan.

Size—Total length: male 115 mm, female 120 mm.

Range—Mutiny Bay, Alaska, to San Diego, California; intertidal.

Distribution in British Columbia—Widespread on sandy beaches of Vancouver Island and the southern mainland. Usually where there is some protection from heavy surf.

Axiopsis spinulicauda

Pagurus samuelis

Pagurus hemphilli

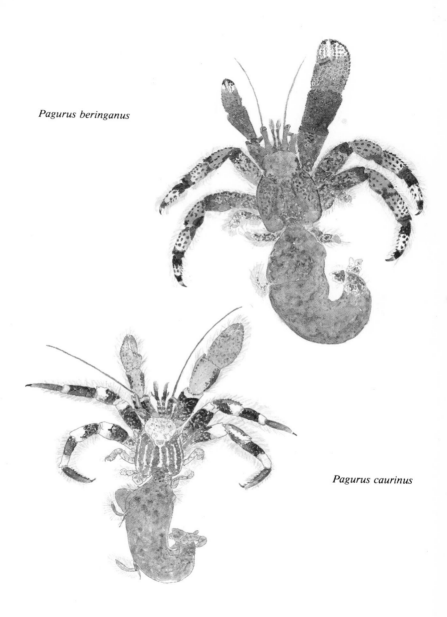

Pagurus beringanus

Pagurus caurinus

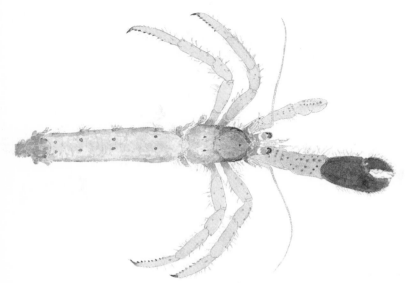

Orthopagurus minimus

Elassochirus gilli

Oedignathus inermis

Placetron wosnessenski

Petrolisthes eriomerus

Petrolisthes cinctipes

Pachycheles rudis

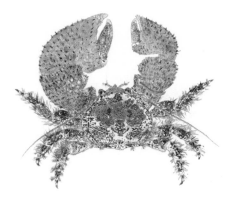

Pachycheles pubescens

Pugettia gracilis

Mimulus foliatus

Scyra acutifrons

Telmessus cheiragonus

Hemigrapsus nudus

Pinnixa faba

Hemigrapsus oregonensis

Pinnixa littoralis

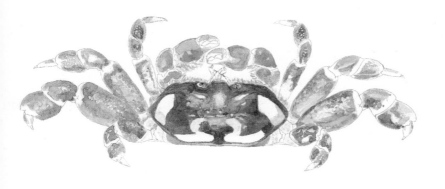

Pinnixa tubicola

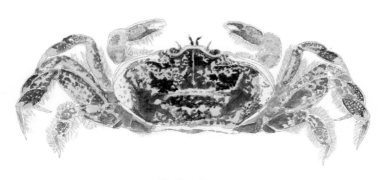

Pinnixa eburna

Scleroplax granulata

Fabia subquadrata

SECTION ANOMURA

Key to Families

1. Crab-like. Abdomen bent under body. Last pair of walking legs small and hidden under edge of carapace...............................2

1. Not crab-like. Abdomen may or may not be bent under body. Last pair of walking legs may or may not be small and hidden...........3

2. Abdomen asymmetrical without uropods.....................Lithodidae

2. Abdomen symmetrical with uropods.........................Porcellanidae

3. Tail fan modified for use as an anchor within hollow objects. Telson figured for each species. Abdomen usually soft and asymmetrical and not clearly segmented................................4

3. Tail fan not used as an anchor. Abdomen calcified and segmented..6

4. Bases of third maxillipeds close together. Chelipeds alike and subequal ....Diogenidae

4. Bases of third maxillipeds separated. Chelipeds unlike and unequal..5

5. No accessory teeth on *crista dentata* of ischium of third maxilliped. Paired pleopods on 1st and 2nd abdomen of male. Only left gonopore developed in female.............Parapaguridae

5. One or more accessory teeth on *crista dentata*. No paired pleopods on either sex. Paired gonopores in female.............Paguridae

6. Egg-shaped. No chelipeds. Uropods and telson elongate ....Hippidae

6. Somewhat lobster-shaped. Chelipeds elongate but uropods and telson short..7

7. Telson with 1 or 2 sutures. Posterior half of abdomen bent under itself with telson tucked over last abdominal segment ....Chirostylidae

7. Telson with numerous sutures. Abdomen bent upon itself but telson not tucked under......................................Galatheidae

Family LITHODIDAE

Key to Species

8. Rostrum with lateral margins not flared. Ridges on abdomen and chelipeds with knobs on surface *Cryptolithodes typicus*

9. Granular knobs on convex carapace and short, stout walking legs 10

9. No granular knobs on relatively flat carapace and long slender walking legs 11

10. When carpi of chelipeds and 1st walking legs are pressed close together the rounded surfaces form tubes or foramina. Spines on antennal scale on margins only ....*Lopholithodes foraminatus*

10. No such foramina. Spines on antennal scale on dorsal surface as well as on margins ....*Lopholithodes mandtii*

11. Carapace, chelipeds and walking legs scaled ....*Placetron wosnessenskii*

11. Carapace, chelipeds and walking legs spined 12

12. Abdomen with plates of calcified nodules on leathery surface 13

13. Dorsal surface of carapace with large and small spines. Walking legs flattened and with serrate margins *Paralomis verrilli*

13. Dorsal surface of carapace with small spines and granules. Walking legs quadrate with serrate margins *Paralomis multispina*

14. 2nd segment of abdomen composed of separated plates ....*Paralithodes camtschatica*

14. 2nd segment of abdomen composed of fused plates 15

15. Large spines on carapace subequal in size. Rostrum stout with single or bifid tip and dorsal, lateral and ventral spines ....*Lithodes aequispina*

15. Large spines on carapace unequal in size. Rostrum elongate, slender, with bifurcate tips and lateral and ventral spines, but no dorsal ....*Lithodes couesi*

The Genus *Hapalogaster* Brandt 1850

Carapace and appendages somewhat flattened and pubescent with specialized setae. Right cheliped larger than left and both longer than walking legs. Abdomen soft, with some thin calcareous plates on the second segment and on the posterior segments of the male. The female has a group of larger plates on the lateral left side of the abdomen which serve as a type of brood pouch to protect the developing eggs.

Hapalogaster grebnitzkii Schalfeew 1892

Description—Carapace relatively flat, covered with short, soft, capitate setae as well as tufts of longer, stiff, clavate setae. Rostrum broadly triangular with a sharp tip and longer than orbital and antero-lateral teeth which are subequal in length with tips curved toward each other. Margin of carapace behind cervical groove cut into stout teeth, which decrease in size posteriorly. Abdomen setose. Eyestalk short and stout. Antennal base spined. Inner margin of last 2 segments of third maxilliped not inflated. Right cheliped stout with dactyl slightly more than half length of palm. Palm with 3 longitudinal rows of spines, the stout upper row being separated from the other 2 by a flat smooth surface. Fingers stout, spoon-shaped, with finely toothed margins. Ventrally mostly naked with an elongated membranous area at base of fixed finger. Smaller left cheliped similar but without membranous area. Walking legs flattened; all dorsal margins (except those of dactyls) are serrate with stout teeth as are the ventral margins of the meri. Chelipeds and walking legs setose, like the carapace, but with the addition of many long, soft setae on the outer margins.

Colour—Preserved specimen similar to *H. mertensii*. Colour of surface masked by light brown setae. Carapace red and orange; marginal spines with white tips. Branchial area pale blue-grey. Abdomen pale brown. Fingers of chelipeds red with yellow tips and white teeth. Walking legs with patches of red dorsally and orange ventrally, with dactyls red proximally and orange distally; claw dark brown. Antennal flagellum uniform brown. Sternum orange with some red spots.

Habitat—Well adapted to secrete themselves between loose rocks and in rocky crevices.

Size—Carapace of male 23 × 24 mm.

Fig. 16 *Hapalogaster grebnitzkii*: a, male, dorsal view; b, distal segments of third maxilliped.

Range—North Pacific Ocean from Sea of Japan to Alaska and south to the southeast side of Winter Inlet, Pearse Island, British Columbia (54°58.7′N, 130°27.5′W); intertidal to 90 m. California records are not valid (Hart 1980).

Distribution in British Columbia—Known only from the above record.

Hapalogaster mertensii Brandt 1850   Hairy Crab

Description—Carapace relatively flat with soft capitate setae and elongate clavate setae and stiff bristles on tips of spines. Rostrum narrow, pointed, and longer than orbital. Antero-lateral teeth straight and slender and much longer than orbital. Margin of carapace behind cervical groove cut into long slender teeth decreasing in size posteriorly. Antennal base spiny. Eyestalk long and slender. Inner margin of last 2 segments of 3rd maxilliped distinctly inflated. Right cheliped like that of *H. grebnitzkii* but usually has 4 longitudinal rows of spines on palm. Dactyl about ¾ length of palm. Walking legs also similar but marginal teeth longer and more slender and with stiff setae near tips of spines. Abdomen with narrow plates on 2nd segment.

Colour—Carapace brown and red, with a few white spots, and covered with pale yellowish tan or dark brown setae and bristles. Tips of fingers of chelipeds orange and teeth white; other surfaces like the carapace. Walking legs with a dark red band and 2 white bands on the propodus. Dactyl red-brown and pale brown with black claw. Sternum red. Eyestalk pale brown; cornea black with orange flecks. Flagellum of antenna banded with wide brown sections and narrow translucent ones.

Habitat—Usually occur under loose rocks, especially when these are covered with seaweeds. The animals are adept at clinging tightly to the undersurface of rocks and squeezing into narrow crevices. Some are parasitized by the rhizochephalan *Briarosaccus tennellus* which can be seen as an egg-filled sac attached to the ventral abdomen.

Size—Carapace: male 25 × 25 mm; female 22 × 24 mm.

Range—Atka, Aleutian Islands, to Puget Sound, Washington; intertidal to 55 m.

Distribution in British Columbia—Widespread in suitable habitats.

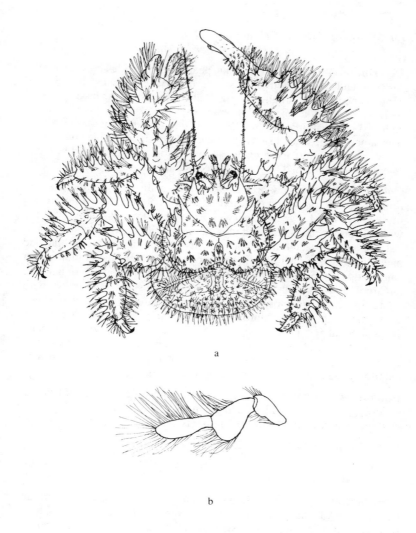

a

b

Fig. 17 *Hapalogaster mertensii*: a, male, dorsal view; b, distal segments of third maxilliped.

Oedignathus inermis (Stimpson 1860)*

Hapalogaster inermis, Hapalogaster brandti, Oedignathus gilli

Description—Carapace somewhat pear-shaped, with short triangular rostrum, and covered with blunt spines and soft setae. Eyestalk short and cone-shaped; cornea small. Chelipeds unequal in size, the larger covered with flat, wart-like masses of granules; fingers spoon-like. Smaller cheliped and walking legs setose with minute sharp granules. Walking legs subcylindrical with short stout dactyls, strong movable spines ventrally, and a strong curved claw. Abdomen soft with basal and terminal segments strengthened by flat calcareous plates.

Colour—Carapace grey-brown and white, with orange granules surrounding white, and with dark red setae and gold bristles. Colour often masked by mud. Large cheliped with ischium and merus blue-grey or tan with red-brown areas; carpus tan with blue-violet or white granules and flat blue granules laterally. Hand brownish with granules violet-blue and pale blue to white laterally; fingers violet and violet-blue granules with smooth tips tan. Small cheliped with ischium and merus white or tan, and a maroon network with a turquoise stripe. Carpus and hand brown with white-tipped orange knobs, red and gold setae, and fingers darker brown with orange tips and dark brown setae. Walking legs white or tan with maroon streaks, green, red and white setae; granular knobs chocolate brown with white tips; dactyl maroon and deep yellow with black spines and claw. Eyestalk brown and white, with cornea black but covered with red film. Base of antenna red and brown; acicle orange and flagellum tan.

Habitat—Open coast in rocky crevices, abandoned sea urchin holes, under kelp holdfasts and between green anemones, such as *Anthopleura xanthogrammica,* and California mussels, *Mytilus californianus.*

Size—Carapace: male 30 × 25 mm; female 22 × 20 mm.

Range—Northwestern Pacific (Japan), Unalaska, Alaska, to Pacific Grove, California; intertidal to 15 m.

Distribution in British Columbia—Outer coasts of Queen Charlotte Islands and Vancouver Island. I have taken them as far east as China Beach on southern Vancouver Island, but the only record for the Strait of Georgia is apparently Porlier Pass where they were found from 5–15 m. (Neil McDaniel *pers. comm.* 1978).

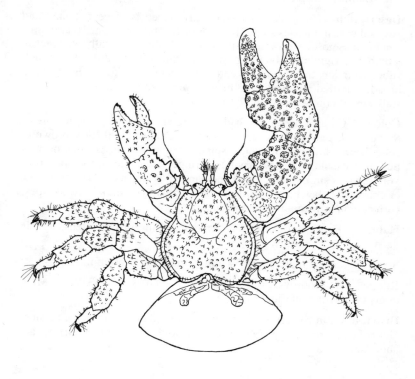

Fig. 18   *Oedignathus inermis*: male, dorsal view.

Acantholithodes hispidus (Stimpson 1860)
Dermaturus hispidus

Description—Carapace somewhat pear-shaped; surface flattened and covered with numerous small spines dorsally and larger ones marginally. Chelipeds setose, with many spines both large and small; subequal in length but right usually much stouter than left. Walking legs stout, subequal in length to chelipeds and similarly armed. Abdomen short and broad, calcified anteriorly and bearing many small setose spines. Eyestalk small, cone-shaped and cornea oval.

Colour—Carapace varying shades of brown with opaque white areas. Spines dark red-brown, orange or white. Chelipeds greenish brown or chocolate with grey-blue bands; spines dark red, orange, white or mottled. Large hand orange with wine red fingers, white teeth and black tips. Walking legs similarly coloured and banded, with dactyl dark red-brown or chocolate; claw black. Eyestalk light brown with dark brown stripes; cornea orange with a black pigment spot.

Habitat—Rocky or muddy areas. Predator of shrimp and often caught in deep-water prawn traps.

Size—Carapace: male 62 × 64 mm; female 49 × 50 mm.

Range—Off Moorovskoy Bay, Alaska (Albatross Stn. 3319), to Monterey, California; interidal to 135 m.

Distribution in British Columbia—Recorded mostly from the Strait of Georgia but probably widespread in localities where shrimp are abundant.

Fig. 19 *Acantholithodes hispidus*: male, dorsal view.

Phyllolithodes papillosus Brandt 1849

Description—Carapace triangular, granulate with rounded, strawberry-like knobs, with 2 depressed areas on either side of cardiac region and with narrow, blunt, projections on lateral margins. Rostrum with a rounded crest terminating in 2 blunt horns and a large spine between eyes ventrally. Eyestalk short and spinulose; cornea slightly dilated. Acicle of antenna with 3 smooth spatulate processes. Chelipeds and walking legs subequal in length and covered with numerous long, flattened, granular, papillate projections, as well as smaller vermiform protruberances and tufts of setae on the hands. Dactyls of walking legs short with stout movable spines ventrally and curved claws.

Colour—Carapace muddy or greenish brown with dark red ridges and depressions and patches of white and yellow (posteriorly orange) and granules turquoise. Chelipeds dark brown with turquoise granules and papillae; hand reddish brown; fingers yellow distally; teeth white and tips dark; ventrally colours lighter and tinged with pink. Walking legs light brown with dark brown papillae; distal half of propodus white; dactyl with dark grey papillae on dark red and with pale orange band distally; claw dark red. Eyestalk blue-grey; cornea orange. Antennal flagellum orange. Abdomen light and dark red, dark brown, and white.

Habitat—Intertidal and subtidal on rocky areas.

Size—Carapace: male 90 × 90 mm; female 50 × 60 mm.

Range—Dutch Harbor, Unalaska, to San Miguel Island, California (34°00′45′55″N, 120°15′00″–16′30″W); intertidal to 183 m.

Distribution in British Columbia—Widespread in suitable areas.

Fig. 20 *Phyllolithodes papillosus*: male, dorsal view.

Rhinolithodes wosnessenskii Brandt 1849

Description—Carapace triangular with scattered granules and a deep semicircular depression surrounding a smooth rounded cardiac area; lateral margins are cut into triangular teeth. Rostrum short and blunt with upturned spined horn ventrally. Eyestalk long and slender, dorsally spined; cornea small. Acicle of antenna elongate and armed with long sharp spines. Chelipeds and walking legs subequal in length, covered with spines and long curved bristles and a membrane which swells on the distal half and under magnification looks like the finger of a glove. Fingers not spined. Dactyls of walking legs short with movable spines ventrally and a sharp, curved claw. Abdomen composed of close-fitting plates, covered with small granules and spines on margins.

Colour—Carapace light brown with base of rostrum orange, depressed area orange and white, granules white, light brown or maroon and lateral teeth white. Chelipeds white with orange, maroon and reddish brown patches with grey-green spines covered with dark red, fading to light brown, setae; hands grey with pink to white fingers with black tips. Walking legs white with maroon and grey spots, grey spines and reddish setae; propodus with proximal white band; dactyl dark to pale grey; claw black. Eyestalk pale brown with four stripes of dark brown; cornea grey-black. Antennal acicle with fine maroon stripes; flagellum brown. Abdomen brown, white and orange.

Habitat—Subtidal; on rocky or gravel bottoms.

Size—Carapace: male 59 × 64 mm; female 50 × 57 mm.

Range—Kodiak, Alaska, to Crescent City, California; from 6 to 73 m.

Distribution in British Columbia—Widespread but relatively rarely collected.

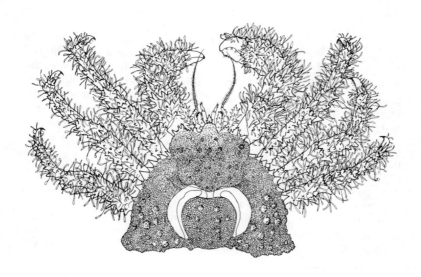

Fig. 21 *Rhinolithodes wosnessenskii*: male, dorsal view.

The Genus *Cryptolithodes* Brandt 1849

Carapace much wider than long, high in the middle and laterally produced into wide expansions so that appendages can be completely concealed. Flattened abdomen triangular and divided into plates, the whole fitting into a depression of the sternum.

Cryptolithodes sitchensis Brandt 1853   Turtle or Umbrella Crab

Description—Carapace surface smooth and about 1½ times as wide as long in males, less in females; medially convex with central longitudinal crest; anterior margins undulated and expanded almost as far forward as rostrum which broadens distally. Eyestalk cone-shaped with small cornea. Antennal scales leaf-like. Chelipeds unequal in size, smooth, and with short setae on inner margins of fingers. Walking legs much compressed with sharp dorsal margins; dactyl short with ventral movable spines and sharp, curved claw. Abdomen of female wider than that of male.

Colour—Carapace with unusually broad range of colour; small individuals are often white or pale brown, and males of any size may be scarlet. Otherwise combinations of all shades of orange, pink, red-brown, green, grey, purple and white occur. One colour may predominate or there may be a mixture with spots, streaks, or a pattern of finely etched, usually symmetrical, lines. Appendages and ventral surfaces mostly white. Chelipeds and walking legs usually have tinges of tan or brown. Eyestalk white; cornea black. Antennal flagellum banded in light and dark brown.

Habitat—Intertidal, especially on wave-washed, seaweed-covered rocks in sheltered crevices, where rock surfaces are covered with colourful growths among which the crabs blend. The tendency to remain motionless also helps them to survive predation. Feed on calcareous algae, *Corallina*, *Calliarthron* and *Bossiella*.

Size—Carapace: male 65 × 90 mm; female 68 × 87 mm.

Range—Sitka, Alaska, to Point Loma, California; intertidal to 17 m.

Distribution in British Columbia—Common in cold-water areas of British Columbia, but I have no records from the Strait of Georgia.

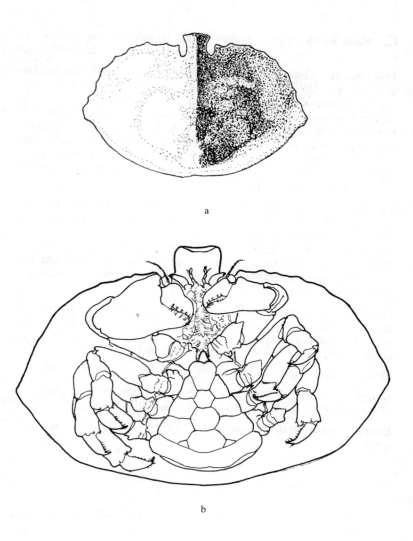

a

b

Fig. 22 *Cryptolithodes sitchensis*, male carapace: a, dorsal view; b, ventral view.

Cryptolithodes typicus Brandt 1849   Butterfly Crab, Turtle Crab, Umbrella Crab

Description—Carapace surface slightly rugose; male more than twice as wide as long, female about 1½ times as wide as long; margins faintly scalloped; a median dorsal ridge and small knobs and elevations laterally. Rostrum sub-rectangular but narrowing distally and sloping downwards. Chelipeds unequal in size; hand broad and flattened, with many knobs and ridges. Abdomen only slightly asymmetrical and with small plates which have upturned edges. Antennal scales leaf-like. Eyestalk cone-shaped; cornea small. Capitate setae on appendages and ventral surfaces produce a somewhat velvet-like surface.

Colour—Carapace varies greatly; small individuals are usually white but larger ones have a tremendous range of colour, mostly brilliant. One colour may predominate or may be combined with others in mottled, streaked or pebbled patterns. Chelipeds and walking legs usually brown with white dorsal margins. Antennal flagellum usually banded in dark and light brown. Ventral surfaces light coloured with a few streaks or spots of bright colour.

Habitat—Subtidal or rarely low intertidal; in crevices or the base of eelgrass on rocky areas well hidden by seaweed. They blend well into the uneven, encrusted rocky habitat and do not move until touched. They eat calcareous algae as well as encrusting animals.

Size—Carapace: male 41 × 75 mm; female 49 × 80 mm.

Range—Amchitka Island, Alaska, to Santa Rosa Island, California (34°01′15″–45′5″N, 120°00′14″–30″W); intertidal to 45 m.

Distribution in British Columbia—Occur in both exposed and sheltered coasts.

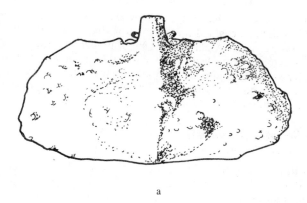

a

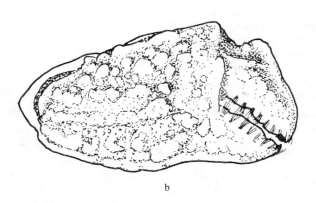

b

Fig. 23 *Cryptolithodes typicus*: a, male carapace, dorsal view; b, hand, outer face.

The Genus *Lopholithodes* Brandt 1848

Carapace broader than long, convex above with granular knobs and rounded protuberances and a smooth, wart-like knob on either side of median gastrict area. Anterior margins of branchial region extended to cover bases of walking legs. Antennal acicle triangular with marginal spines. The knobby chelipeds and walking legs fit together when folded, hence the common name Box Crab. Juveniles have proportionately larger and more prominent elevations on the dorsal surfaces.

Lopholithodes foraminatus (Stimpson 1859)
Echinocerus foraminatus

Description—Carapace convex; covered with small granules and spines on high points of dorsal surface and on margins. Rostrum a sharp upturned spine with several smaller spines crowded above the base. Eyestalk subequal in length to rostrum with small sharp spines on dorsal surface; cornea small and ventrally placed. Antennal acicle with upright spines on lateral margins only. Chelipeds and walking legs subequal in length with numerous granulated spines and tufts of setae on all exposed area. Chelipeds each with lateral extensions on inner dorsal margins of merus; carpus and propodus upcurved so that mouth parts are protected. On outer margin of each cheliped carpus a smooth deep semicircular sinus coincides with a similar flatter structure on carpus of each 1st walking leg. When the appendages are pressed together a nearly circular hole, or foramen, results. Larger cheliped, with fingers armed with molar-like teeth for crushing; smaller cheliped has small sharp teeth for cutting; all fingers have corneous tips. Lateral surfaces of walking legs smooth so that they fit together tightly; dactyl short and relatively slender with granulated spines and a sharp claw. Abdomen with knob-covered plates.

Colour—Carapace red-brown with purplish tinge and white areas, particularly in the depressions. Smooth, paired, knobs dark-red. Chelipeds dorsally white, tan and mottled with red; fingers orange or red, tips white, as well as teeth, and corneous tips dark brown. Ventral surfaces mostly white with some patches of red and purple. Foramen white, lined with purple streaks. Walking legs white with red-brown dorsally; propodus with narrow band of white granules distally; dactyl red-brown and

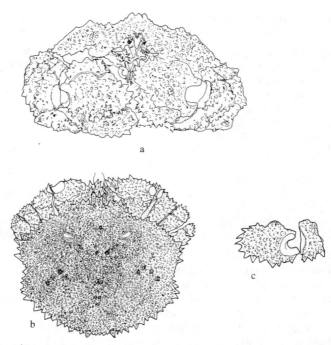

Fig. 24 *Lophólithodes foraminatus*, male: a, anterior view; b, dorsal view; c, foramen.

white distally, with brown claw. Eyestalk white ventrally, pale brown dorsally and reddish or white spines; cornea orange brown. Antennal flagellum tan. Abdomen with violet patches and some red-brown nodules.

Habitat—Muddy bottom.

Size—Carapace: male 165 × 185 mm; female 145 × 175 mm.

Range—North of Banks Island, Hecate Strait, British Columbia (53°40′N, 130°30′W), to San Diego, California; intertidal to 547 m.

Distribution in British Columbia—Common in muddy areas; often caught by draggers.

Lopholithodes mandtii Brandt 1849　　　　　Box Crab
Echinocercus cibarius, Ctenorhinus setimanus

Description—Carapace covered with granules of different sizes, covering small knobs and blunt spines on the margins. Cone-shaped elevations over gastric, cardiac and branchial areas. Rostrum blunt spine bearing 3 knobs above the base. Eyestalk small, shorter than rostrum, covered with many needle-like spines; cornea small and ventrally placed. Antennal acicle with dorsal surface and lateral margins coverd with smooth slender spines. Chelipeds each with extensions on inner dorsal margins of merus; carpus and propodus with upcurved spines so that the mouth parts are covered when chelipeds are withdrawn. The exposed areas are covered with large, granulated, blunt spines and knobs. Teeth of larger hand, large and molar-like and those of smaller hand, small and numerous. Fingers with corneous ring at tip. Walking legs with lateral faces smooth, so that they fit closely together, and exposed areas are heavily armed like the chelipeds; dactyl short, with a strong claw. Abdomen composed of plates well armed with granulated knobs.

Colour—Carapace scarlet, violet or cobalt-blue, with high points and knobs orange. Some granules brown and the smooth knobs on either side of gastric area are dark red. Chelipeds and walking legs yellow, orange, red and blue. Cutting teeth of chelipeds white and setae dark brown; tips of fingers black. Abdomen yellow, red and blue. Eyestalk red-brown with light spines; cornea orange or red. Antennal flagellum red and faintly banded.

Habitat—Usually subtidal rocky area. Sea Urchins are eaten. Has been observed feeding on sea anemones (Brent Cooke, *pers. comm.*).

Size—Carapace: male 200 × 270 mm.

Range—Sitka, Alaska, to Monterey, California; intertidal to 137 m.

Distribution in British Columbia—Not uncommon but the activities of SCUBA divers have probably reduced the numbers of large individuals.

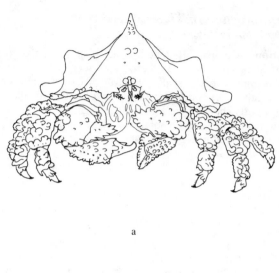

a

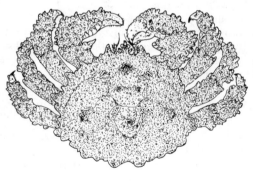

b

Fig. 25 *Lopholithodes mandtii*: a, juvenile, anterior view; b, male, dorsal view.

Placetron wosnessenskii Schalfeew 1892*
Lepeopus forcipatus

Description—Carapace flattened, wider posteriorly than long, covered with curved protuberances bordered anteriorly with short bristles and giving the impression of scales. Rostrum triangular and curved downward. Eyestalk short and protected by rostrum. Chelipeds slender, subequal and slightly shorter than walking legs, scaled, with forward-pointing sharp teeth on inner margin of merus and carpus. Hand with spoon-shaped fingers. Walking legs long and stout, scaled, and dorsal margin of merus irregularly serrate with sharp teeth. Ventral distal propodus with needle-like movable spines; dactyl with a row of strong movable spines and curved sharp claws. Anterior dorsal part of abdomen flat with some thin calcareous plates which are scaled. The rest of the abdomen is rounded and soft except for a calcareous telson. In the female there is a calcified area on the left side supporting the pleopods.

Colour—Carapace medially red-brown and laterally grey with dark brown scales. Chelipeds with red-brown or orange scales and grey or turquoise teeth with white tips. Hand orange and tan with dark red-brown area on dorsal palm and some turquoise streaks on fingers. Walking legs: ischium red-brown; merus orange-brown with red-brown and turquoise bands distally and a small patch of scarlet at junction of carpus which is pale turquoise dorsally and orange ventrally with a dark red band medially; propodus similar but with two dark red bands, and a terminal orange band with black ventral spines; dactyl dark red to orange with spines and claw black. Calcified parts of abdomen light brown, the rest olive green. Eyestalk dark brown; cornea brick red. Antennal flagellum red.

Habitat—Subtidal in rocky area. Very quick moving; therefore, rarely caught in dredges. SCUBA divers can chase them so more have been caught in recent years. Often associated with sea anemones, *Metridium senile*. The spines on the tips of the walking legs may be an adaptation to life in such a habitat.

Size—Carapace: male 61 × 72 mm; female 50 × 53 mm.

Range—Aleutian Islands, Alaska, to Puget Sound, Washington; intertidal to 110 m.

Distribution in British Columbia—Widespread.

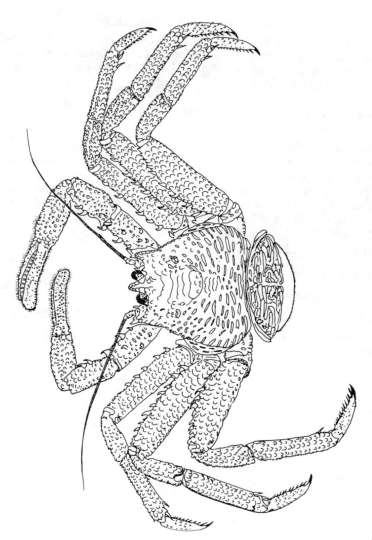

Fig. 26 *Placetron wosnessenskii*: male, dorsal view.

The Genus *Paralomis* White 1856

Carapace granular and/or spined. A stout spine on gastric area. Rostrum with 3 sharp projections. Walking legs either flattened or angular with rows of spines on margins. Abdomen of nodule-covered plates separated by membranous area. Usually abyssal.

Paralomis verrilli (Benedict 1894)
Pristopus verrilli

Description—Carapace slightly longer than wide, with small granules and spines of varying sizes; large spines on elevated areas and lateral margins. Eyestalk stout with small granules and oval cornea ventrally. Antennal peduncle with slender spines. Chelipeds much shorter than walking legs, which are stout, somewhat flattened and margined, ventrally and dorsally, with rows of large spines with scattered small spines. Abdomen with small spines and many rod-shaped nodules.

Colour—Unrecorded but probably scarlet.

Habitat—Deep water.

Size—Carapace: male 112 × 102 mm.

Range—Sea of Okhotsk, to Cortez Bank, California; 1238–2379 m.

Distribution in British Columbia—West of Tasu Sound, Queen Charlotte Is. (52°40–55′N, 132°12–54′W); 1737–1829 m.

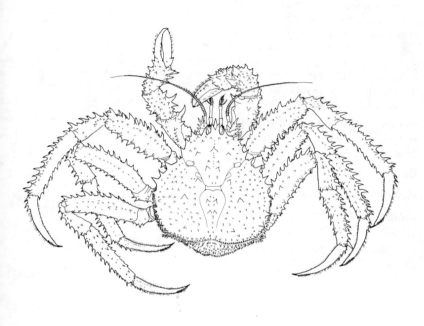

Fig. 27 *Paralomis verrilli*: female, dorsal view.

Paralomis multispina (Benedict 1894)
Leptolithodes multispinus

Description—Carapace subequal in length and width, with convex areas; covered with small spines and nodules, and margined with larger, slender spines. There is also a large spine on the crest of the gastric area and on each branchial area. Eyestalk stout with small spines dorsally and oval cornea ventrally. Acicle of antenna with long slender spines. Chelipeds of juveniles subequal in length to walking legs and, in adults, shorter than walking legs. Right hand stout with swollen palm and armed with long slender spines. Walking legs slender and covered with many sharp spines in rows on ridges with flat area between, especially obvious on the carpi and propodi; dactyl short with sharp, curved claw.

Colour—Carapace scarlet with spines dark and nodules light. Chelipeds and walking legs scarlet with lighter-coloured spines and tips of fingers. Eyestalk scarlet; cornea black. Antennal flagellum scarlet.

Habitat—Deep sea mud.

Size—Carapace: male 80 × 78 mm.

Range—Shumagin Bank, Alaska, to San Diego, California; from 830 to 1665 m.

Distribution in British Columbia—West of Vancouver and Queen Charlotte Islands; from 951 to 1603 m.

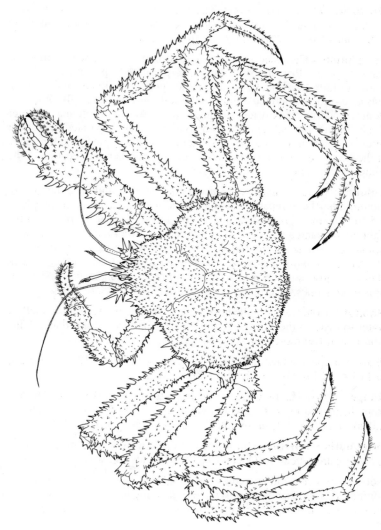

Fig. 28 *Paralomis multispina*: male, dorsal view.

Paralithodes camtschatica (Tilesius 1815)

Maja camtschatica, Lithodes spinosissimus,
L. camtschatica, Paralithodes rostrofalcatus

King Crab,
Alaska King Crab

Description—Carapace subovate and surface covered with numerous conical spines. Rostrum with long, sharp-pointed tip, a median dorsal spine, usually bifid, and 2 small lateral spines. Chelipeds and walking legs also spined; chelipeds shorter than walking legs. Eyestalk short and stout with cornea mostly anterior and ventral. Acicle of antenna a slender spine. 2nd abdominal segment composed of 5 plates separated by distinct sutures. Young individuals have longer and sharper spines and the shape of the carapace is somewhat different but the number and location of the spines is the same.

Colour—Varies considerably according to size and whether or not moulting has been recent. Carapace of adults brownish red or purplish-red and cream or greenish-white. Spines mostly deeper in colour, with a light dorsal band and a dark tip. Chelipeds and walking legs cream with patches and streaks of red dorsally. Fingers with white teeth and dark tips. Dactyls of walking legs with lateral streaks of red and corneous dark claws. Ventral surface mostly light with some red patches and light-tipped red spines. Juveniles orange overall.

Habitat—Cold waters of the northern Pacific Ocean. Migrate to shallow water to mate in the spring. Young inhabit shallower water than adults, who may travel more than 100 miles in their lifetime.

Size—Carapace: male 227 × 283 mm; female 195 × 213 mm. Weight to 11 kg (24 lbs.) of which about 25% is meat.

Range—North Pacific Ocean from Japan to northern British Columbia; from 14 to 366 m. A tagged individual travelled 556 km (300 nautical miles) in 290 days. Can migrate 13 km (7 miles) per day.

Distribution in British Columbia—Northern British Columbia. Some spawning areas near the Queen Charlotte Islands and adjacent mainland.

Notes—Two-year-old juveniles are gregarious and form aggregations composed of thousands of individuals who cling upon each other to form ball-shaped pods. Apparently this is done for protection against predators.

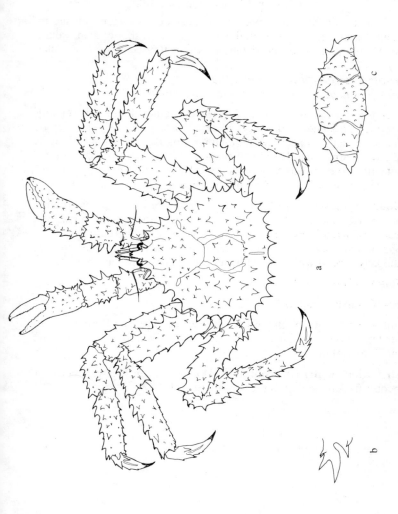

Fig. 29 *Paralithodes camtschatica*: a, male, dorsal view; b, rostrum, lateral view; c, 2nd abdominal segment.

The Genus *Lithodes* Latreille 1806

Carapace subcircular, armed with stout spines. Rostrum elongate and spined. Cardiac region depressed. Chelipeds much shorter than walking legs. Median plate of second abdominal segment fused with lateral plates.

Lithodes aequispina Benedict 1894
Lithodes aequispinus, Paralithodes longirostris

Description—Carapace round with conical spines, longest marginally. Rostrum with spines: 2 dorsally, 4 laterally and 1 ventrally; tip may be bifid; subequal chelipeds shorter than walking legs, which are elongate and have sharp, broad-based spines on all surfaces. Eyestalk short and stout with cornea mostly ventral. Antennal acicle small and tipped with 2 or 3 sharp spines. 2nd segment of abdomen spined and entire.

Colour—Carapace reddish tan and dark red anteriorly. Spines with red base, a light band and dark brown tips. Chelipeds reddish tan and streaked with red-brown. Spines light, fingers orange and cutting teeth on finger of right hand white; those of left brown. Walking legs tan and light mahogany; dactyl with terminal bands orange and tips dark brown.

Habitat—Continental shelf.

Size—Carapace: male 187 × 195 mm.

Range—Japan, Sea of Okhotsk (northwest Pacific), and Bering Sea, to Ucluelet, Vancouver Island (48°45′N, 125°20′W), British Columbia; from 77 to 730 m.

Distribution in British Columbia—Records from the west coast of Vancouver Island and Queen Charlotte Sound.

Fig. 30 *Lithodes aequispina*: a, male, dorsal view; b, rostrum, lateral view.

a

b

Lithodes couesi Benedict 1894

Descripton—Carapace margined with sharp spines with smaller conical spines on dorsal areas and on chelipeds and walking legs. Rostrum with bifid tip and a pair of lateral spines. Subequal chelipeds shorter than walking legs. Eyestalk small; cornea terminal. Acicle of antenna small with slender spines. Abdomen not spined; 2nd segment composed of fused plates. Juveniles strikingly different due to the proportions of the body and length of spines.

Colour—Carapace rose pink with white grooves. Spines red with yellow tips and some small white granules. Chelipeds crimson with white joints; fingers with white teeth and yellow setae. Walking legs crimson with white spots and knobs at junctions; claws yellow with dark tips. Eyestalk red with pink band; cornea red-brown or black. Antennule crimson; flagella orange. Antenna base pink with red spines, the rest crimson, including flagellum. Juveniles scarlet.

Habitat—Dredged from mud or boulders in deep water.

Size—Carapace: male 105 × 81 mm.

Range—Bering Sea to off San Diego, California; from 258 to 1829 m.

Distribution in British Columbia—West of Vancouver Island, Tasu Sound, Engelfield Bay, Queen Charlotte Islands, and Dixon Entrance.

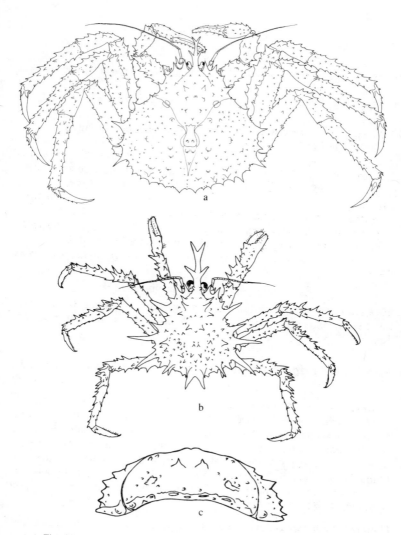

Fig. 31 *Lithodes couesi*: a, male, dorsal view; b, juvenile, dorsal view; c, 2nd abdominal segment.

Family PORCELLANIDAE

Key to Species

1. Chelipeds subequal in size; broad, smooth and flat. Carpus elongated ... 2
1. Chelipeds unequal in size; thick and rough surfaced. Carpus stout ... 3
2. Carpus of cheliped with margins parallel and twice a long as wide. Meri of legs setose. Tip of third maxilliped blue ... *Petrolisthes eriomerus*
2. Carpus of cheliped widest proximally and less than twice as long as wide. Meri of legs not setose. Tip of third maxilliped red ... *Petrolisthes cinctipes*
3. Surface of hand rough, sparsely setose, with a large bare knob on median distal part. Telson of 5 plates ... *Pachycheles rudis*
3. Surface of hand uniformly granular and covered by a dense pubescence. Telson of 7 plates ... *Pachycheles pubescens*

The Genus *Petrolisthes* Stimpson 1858

Carapace round in outline, front prominent. Chelipeds large, subequal, with hands broad and flattened. Walking legs somewhat flattened. Telson of 7 plates.

Petrolisthes eriomerus Stimpson 1871* Flat-topped Crab, Porcellanid Crab

Description—Carapace with granules anteriorly, posterior area striated, and few, if any, setae. Chelipeds large and flat; carpus about twice as long as wide, with small rough granules, a median longitudinal crest and a serrate outer margin ending in a tooth distally. Large tuft of dense pubescence at base of finger. Walking legs with fine plumose and non-plumose setae scattered on surface in tufts. Male with a pair of gonopods on 2nd abdominal segment. Female with uniramous paired pleopods on segments 4 and 5.

Colour—Granules on carapace red-brown or white (giving a pebbled appearance) with blue tinges in the grooves and a blue and white "comma" on either side of cardiac region. Chelipeds with dark and light

Fig. 32 *Petrolisthes eriomerus*: male, dorsal view.

red granules with orange areas and blue-white patches at junctions of segments. Walking legs mahogany brown with 2 patches of yellow on merus, none on carpus, and a red and a yellow band proximally and a yellow distally on propodus with red, brown and yellow on dactyl and a dark brown claw. Abdomen red-brown and blue. Antennal flagellum greyish green. Outer maxillipeds red, brown and blue, with both surfaces of last 2 articles bright blue.

Habitat—Intertidal, under rocks.

Size—Carapace: male 19 × 19 mm; female 19 × 19 mm.

Range—Klokachef Island, Chichagof Island (57°25′N, 135°52′W), Alaska,to La Jolla, California; intertidal to 86 m.

Distribution in British Columbia—Common, but possibly less abundant where in competition with *P. cinctipes* on outer coasts.

Petrolisthes cinctipes (Randall 1839)*

Porcellana cinctipes, P. rupicola, Petrolisthes rupicolus

Description—Carapace with fine granules and striae but no setae. Chelipeds large, flattened and finely granulate dorsally. Carpus 1½ to twice as long as wide, large tuft of soft setae ventrally at base of fingers. Walking legs with merus and carpus almost naked but propodus and dactyl with tufts of short setae. Male with paired gonopods on 2nd segment of abdomen. Female with paired pleopods on segments 4 and 5.

Colour—Granules on carapace red or dark brown with blue areas and fine grey-blue striae laterally and a blue and white "comma" on either side of cardiac area. Cheliped granules dark brown, red-brown, red, yellow, blue or white forming patches and striations but giving an overall pebbled look. Walking legs dark brown with small blue patches; merus with yellow band distally; propodus with yellow median band; dactyl yellow with narrow brown band and light brown claw. Abdomen dark and light brown and blue. Outer maxilliped dark brown with last 2 articles scarlet. Eyestalk dark brown; cornea dark grey or black.

Habitat—Intertidal among rocks and in mussel beds on open coasts. It is often found higher up on the beach than *P. eriomerus.*

Size—Carapace: male 21 × 20 mm; female 24 × 24 mm.

Range—Welcome Harbour, Porcher Island (54°0.05'N, 130°40'W), British Columbia, to Santa Barbara and offshore islands, California; intertidal to 64 m.

Distribution in British Columbia—Common on outer coast east to Port Renfrew; no authenticated records for the Strait of Georgia.

The Genus *Pachycheles* Stimpson 1858

Carapace circular in outline with rounded front. Chelipeds large and stout, one larger than the other. Hand with fixed finger shorter than dactyl and carpus short and stout. Walking legs of moderate length and somewhat flattened. Telson of 5 or 7 plates. Pleopods of male may be reduced or lacking.

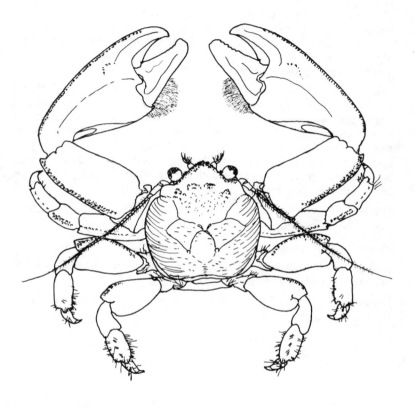

Fig. 33 *Petrolisthes cinctipes*: male, dorsal view.

Pachycheles rudis Stimpson 1858*

Description—Carapace about as broad as long, convex with flat granules; front with short stiff setae. Chelipeds rugose and granular with a large granulated knob at base of fixed finger. Chelipeds and walking legs with setae, some of which are plumose. Telson of 5 plates. Male with a pair of gonopods on 2nd segment of abdomen. Female with paired uniramous pleopods on segments 3 to 5.

Colour—Carapace mottled and striated with grey, brown and white and some with blue granules; white "commas" on branchial region. Chelipeds greenish brown with grey and bluish granules. There is an orange spot at junction of carpus and propodus which is hidden when bent; fingers blue with white tips. Walking legs reticulated brown, grey and white; dactyls banded with dark grey and white; claws brown. Eyestalk dark grey; cornea black with red rim. Abdomen grey-green, tan and white with light median streak.

Habitat—Usually found intertidally under stones, in holdfasts of kelp or any well-protected area or crevice. Male and female cohabit.

Size—Carapace: male 19 × 19 mm; female 18.5 × 18.5 mm.

Range—Kodiak, Alaska, to Bahia de la Magdalena, Baja California, Mexico; intertidal to 29 m.

Distribution in British Columbia—Found on the open coast and, rarely, as far east as Victoria.

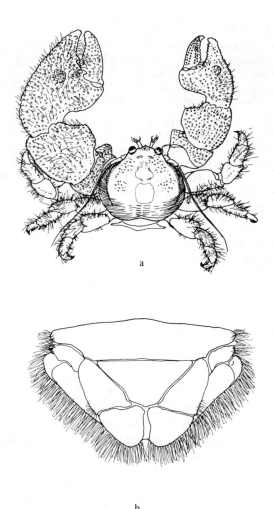

a

b

Fig. 34 *Pachycheles rudis*: a, male, dorsal view; b, tail fan.

101

Pachycheles pubescens Holmes 1900*

Description—Carapace convex and slightly broader than long; front masked by dense pubescence, longest medially. Chelipeds with granules nearly covered by dense pubescence and longer bristles. Telson of 7 plates. Male with paired gonopods on 2nd segment of abdomen. Female with paired uniramous pleopods on segments 3 to 5.

Colour—Carapace white, dappled with brown, grey and purple, with a blue and tan "comma" on each branchial area. Cheliped colour masked by mud-coloured pubescence; granules pale violet. Finger tips may be pink. Walking legs with merus blue and brown with variations in depth of colour which creates a banded appearance. Propodus and dactyl with distal white bands. Eyestalk dark brown and white; cornea red-brown with black centre.

Habitat—Rocky areas, occasionally intertidally but usually subtidally on exposed coast. Male and female cohabit.

Size—Carapace: male 18 × 18.5 mm; female 17 × 17.5 mm.

Range—Bush Rock, Huston Inlet, south side Skincuttle Inlet, Queen Charlotte Islands (52°18′N, 131°16.5′W), British Columbia, to Thurloe Head, Baja California, Mexico; intertidal to 55 m.

Distribution in British Columbia—Open coast and, rarely, as far east as Victoria.

Superfamily PAGURIDEA
Family DIOGENIDAE
Key To Species

1. Eyestalk about one half length of shield; antennal flagellum sparsely setose. Hands with more than half cutting surface composed of dark corneous teeth. Brood pouch of female narrow, sub-triangular in shape .... *Paguristes turgidus*
1. Eyestalk nearly as long as shield; antennal flagellum with two rows of long, dense, plumose setae. Hands with few dark corneous teeth. Brood pouch of female semi-rectangular .... *Paguristes ulreyi*

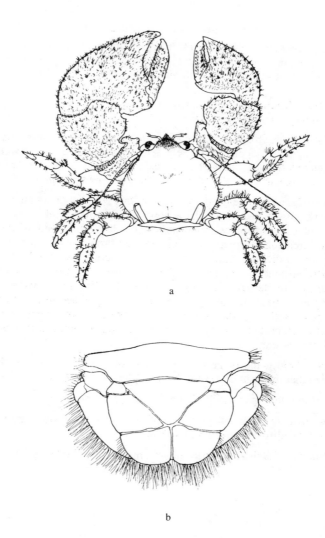

a

b

Fig. 35   *Pachycheles pubescens*: a, male, dorsal view; b, tail fan.

The Genus *Pagurites* Dana 1851

Chelipeds subequal. Bases of 3rd maxillipeds close together. Male with paired gonopods on 1st and 2nd abdominal segments. A brood pouch at base of 4th pleopod of female.

Pagurites turgidus (Stimpson 1857)
Clibanarius turgidus, Eupagurus turgidus

Description—Crab spiny and setose with many sharp corneous-tipped spines. Antennal flagellum sparsely setose ventrally. Eyestalk slender and about ½ length of shield. Hand with dark corneous teeth on more than half of cutting surfaces. Brood pouch of female subtriangular.

Colour—Carapace shield rust-red and yellow, with lateral and posterior areas dark red with white streaks. Cheliped red-brown, pink, cream and white, with bases of spines cream and tips black. Cutting teeth white and corneous areas dark brown. Walking legs red-brown, white and cream; dactyls red to orange; claws black. Abdomen cream with red reticulations. Brood pouch translucent white, covering scarlet eggs. Antennal base white, with narrow wine-red stripe dorsally; flagellum dark red and pink. Antennal base orange with fine red spots; flagellum white with dark red stripe dorsally. Eyestalk opaque white with dark red stripes laterally and ventrally; scale red and orange with white tipped spines; cornea black with gold crescent.

Habitat—Mud, sand or gravel bottom; usually inhabit shells of sufficient size that the crab can withdraw completely.

Size—Shield length: male 17.7 mm; female 11.4 mm.

Range—Chukchi Sea (68°13.5′N, 166°35.8′W), northwest Pacific, to San Diego, California; from 5 to 465 m.

Distribution in British Columbia—Common in suitable habitat.

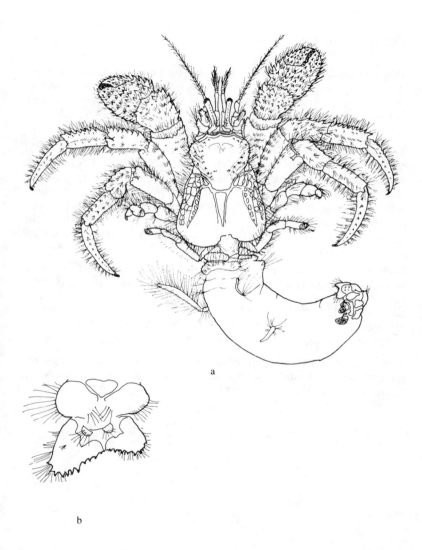

a

b

Fig. 36 *Paguristes turgidus*: a, male, dorsal view; b, telson.

Paguristes ulreyi Schmitt 1921
Paguristes occator

Description—Differs from *P. turgidus* by antennal flagellum being densely setose ventrally and sparsely dorsally, eyestalk proportionately long and more slender, nearly as long as shield and hand with dark corneous teeth only at tips of fingers. Brood pouch of female sub-rectangular.

Colour—Carapace red-brown with 3 irregular lighter stripes on shield and 1 on each branchial area. Chelipeds white with orange, light and dark red bands; fingers pink and white with black tips. Walking legs rust and white, with black claws. Abdomen mottled red and white. Antennule white with dark red streaks and flagellum red ventrally. Antenna pink and red base; flagellum dark red with light areas at joints and setae light coloured. Eyestalk white with dark red, almost black stripes dorso-laterally and ventrally; cornea black.

Habitat—Intertidally in rock crevices on exposed shores and subtidally in rocky and gravelled areas but in shallower water than *P. turgidus*.

Size—Shield length: male 12 mm; female 9.4 mm.

Range—Frederick Island (53°56′N, 133°08.3′W), British Columbia, to Baja California and Gulf of California, Mexico; intertidal to 157 m.

Distribution in British Columbia—Intertidally on the outer coast off Queen Charlotte Islands and subtidally off the outer coast of Vancouver Island.

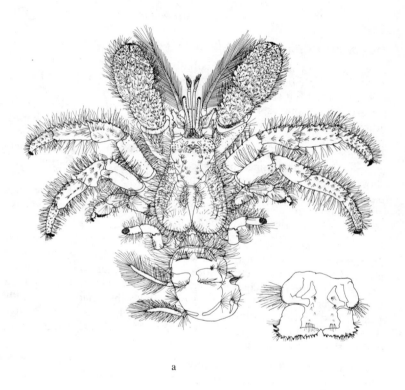

a

b

Fig. 37 *Paguristes ulreyi*: a, male, dorsal view; b, telson.

Family PARAPAGURIDAE

Key to Species

1. Chelipeds covered with a dense pubescence which hides the small sharp granules on the surface. Found only in deep water ....

.... *Parapagurus pilosimanus benedicti*

Parapagurus pilosimanus benedicti de Saint Laurent 1972

Description—Carapace shield slightly wider than long. Eyestalk slender; eyescale may be bifid; cornea little dilated. Right cheliped much larger than left but shorter than walking legs and covered with a dense pubescence of long, soft setae which mask the numerous sharp spiny granules; hand long and wide with short stout fingers. Left cheliped slender, similarly armed with pubescence and sharp granules but fingers elongate. Walking legs long; merus laterally compressed and slender, curved dactyl much longer than other segments the dorsal margins with short stiff setae which increase in length distally; claw small. Male with paired gonopods on 1st and 2nd segments of abdomen. Female with pleopods only on 2nd to 5th side of abdomen and 1 gonopore on the coxa of the left 3rd pereipod (2nd walking leg).

Colour—Carapace shield opaque, light orange, the sides deep red, posterior wine-red with an opaque, white elongated triangle in the cardiac area and whitish areas on either side of this; pubescence white. Abdomen orange and wine-red. Right cheliped with cream pubescence; ischium orange; merus scarlet; carpus pale pink and white; hand white with ventral part of fingers pink. Left cheliped similar but fingers orange dorsally and ventrally. Walking legs orange and scarlet. Eyestalk orange and scarlet; cornea dark brown. Antennal flagellum orange.

Habitat—Deep water on mud bottom; shell often with attached anemones which are believed to emit phosphorescent light.

Size—Shield length: male 13.4 mm.

Range—Alaska to Gulf of Panama; from 415 to 2200 m.

Distribution in British Columbia—Known from six localities in deep water off the outer coast.

a

b

Fig. 38 *Parapagurus pilosimanus benedicti*: a, male, dorsal view; b, telson.

Family PAGURIDAE

Key to Species

1. Carapace almost entirely calcified and spined dorsally ......
   .... *Labidochirus splendescens*
1. Carapace with only shield calcified, smooth and not spined 2
2. Uropods symmetrical and abdomen not coiled. 3
2. Uropods asymmetrical and abdomen coiled 4
3. Telson with median transverse constrictions and cleft terminally. Small. Usually inhabit *Dentalium* shells ....
   .... *Orthopagurus minimus*
3. Telson with neither constriction nor cleft. Usually inhabit
   empty Sabellarid or Serpulid worm tubes. Small ....
   .... *Discorsopagurus schmitti*
4. Right cheliped with carpus and/or palm with outer margin a
   flattened plate. Eyescales with raised margins. 5
4. Right cheliped with a ridge or with outer margins of carpus
   and palm rounded. Eyescales without raised margins 7
5. Chelipeds with smooth surfaces; carpus produced laterally
   and wider than palm 6
5. Chelipeds finely granulate dorsally; large hand and carpus
   much flattened, with sharp lateral margins partly toothed ..
   .... *Elassochirus tenuimanus*
6. Carpus of large cheliped with a row of small spines on the
   proximal central area .... *Elassochirus cavimanus*
6. No such spines on carpus .... *Elassochirus gilli*
7. Eyestalk short and stout; cornea elongate-oval (ovate). Dactyls of walking legs twisted and armed with a dense comb of
   short spines ventrally 8
7. Eyestalk short or long; cornea spherical. Dactyls of walking legs not twisted and ventral spines widely spaced 10
8. Hands with dorsal surface armed with many sharp spines
   and ventral surface smooth .... *Pagurus armatus*
8. Hands with dorsal and ventral surfaces armed with round or
   pointed granules 9

9. Granules with one point. No groove on dactyl of walking legs. Dark red streaks near cutting surface of fingers
.... *Pagurus ochotensis*

9. Most granules with two points. Elongate groove on dactyl of walking legs. No dark red streaks near cutting surface of fingers .... *Pagurus aleuticus*

10. Hands with flat and/or pointed granules on dorsal surface 11

10. Hands with spines or pointed granules on dorsal surface 15

11. Shield of carapace distinctly longer than wide 12

11. Shield little if any longer than wide 13

12. Carpus of right cheliped not swollen ventrally. Left cheliped about ¾ size of right; merus with serrate ventral margin .... *Pagurus samuelis*

12. Carpus of right cheliped swollen ventrally. Left cheliped about ½ size of right; merus with ventral margin not serrate
.... *Pagurus hemphilli*

13. Hands with flat granules evenly distributed over all surfaces
.... *Pagurus granosimanus*

13. Hands with flat or pointed granules, not evenly distributed and few, if any, on ventral surfaces 14

14. Rostrum large and sharp. Merus of large hand with small narrow teeth on distal margin .... *Pagurus hirsutiusculus*

14. Rostrum small and rounded. Merus of large hand with large triangular teeth on distal margin .... *Pagurus beringanus*

15. Dorsal surfaces of large hand with a broad raised triangle with apex at base of dactyl. Small hand with a double row of spines on central ridge; outer part of palm dilated. Eyestalk short and stout; cornea distinctly dilated 16

15. No such distinct broad raised triangle. Small hand rarely with central ridge and palm not dilated. Eyestalk long; cornea not dilated 18

16. Walking legs with dorsal margins of propodi serrate ....
.... *Pagurus tanneri*

16. Walking legs with dorsal margin of propodi not serrate or minutely so 17

17. Large hand with apex of triangle horn-shaped in profile.....
.... *Pagurus cornutus*

17. Large hand with apex of triangle rounded in profile...........
.... *Pagurus confragosus*

18. Hands with small spines and granules. Setae not conspic-
uous.. 24

18. Hands with spines, usually large and with conspicuous
tufts of setae... 19

19. Dactyl and propod of walking legs subequal in length................. 20

19. Dactyl distinctly longer than propod................................ 22

20. Large cheliped with carpus subequal to hand. Sparsely
setose. No serrate margins or walking legs. Eyescale may
be multipointed.. *Pagurus* sp.

20. Large cheliped with carpus not subequal to hand in length.
Densely setose. Some serrate margins on walking legs.
Eyescale with single pointed tip....................................... 21

21. Tufts of stout, stiff setae; do not hide large spines. Antennal
flagellum banded with dark and light coloured segments.
Distal margin of telson deeply cleft and with small straight
teeth .... *Pagurus kennerlyi*

21. Dense tufts of soft setae, some plumose; do hide spines.
Antennal flagellum not banded. Distal margin of telson not
deeply cleft and with stout curved teeth................ *Pagurus caurinus*

22. Dactyls of walking legs with stout movable spines ventrally 23

22. Dactyls of walking legs with minute movable spines ven-
trally.. *Pagurus capillatus*

23. Hands with sharp spines in clearly defined rows dorsally.
Dorsal margin of propodus of right 1st walking leg not
serrate. Eyescale with one point. Antennal flagellum trans-
lucent.. *Pagurus setosus*

23. Hands with scattered small spines dorsally. Dorsal margin
of propodus of right 1st walking leg serrate. Eyescale
usually multipointed. Antennal flagellum translucent with
dark brown bands... *Pagurus quaylei*

24. Carpus of large cheliped relatively stout and widest distally. Outer margin beaded with sharp spines........................ *Pagurus dalli*

24. Carpus of large cheliped elongate, with sides subparallel. Outer margin not indicated by a beading of spines...............
.... *Pagurus stevensae*

Labidochirus splendescens (Owen 1839)
Pagurus splendescens, Eupagurus splendescens

Description—Carapace calcified throughout; shield wider than long, with a distinct rostrum and with some spiny ridges and spines dorsally, and sharp teeth laterally. Posterior part of carapace with scattered spines and ridges; mid-lateral margins of carapace serrate. Eyestalk short; large cornea spherical. Right cheliped slender and slightly longer than left and shorter than walking legs; setose with some marginal and dorsal spines as well as spined scales. Left cheliped similar but more slender with proportionately longer fingers. Walking legs setose, with marginal spines and spined scales on lateral faces; merus wide and laterally compressed; dactyl slender and slightly longer than propodus, with stiff setae on dorsal margin and small movable spines ventrally. 5th pereiopod (last walking leg) without the usual strong rasp of setae found in most hermit crabs. Abdomen small with vestigial or no pleopods in the male.

Colour—Shield with narrow white margins anteriorly and cream with brown reticulations; posteriorly red, yellow-brown and white. Chelipeds with bronze iridescence; ischium red and purplish red; merus with yellow, brown and purple patches and a distal purplish band with white-tipped spines; carpus red with brown spines; hand amethyst, with light-tipped purple-red spines; fixed finger deep purple with white tips and teeth; dactyl pink with red-purple stripe and white teeth. Walking legs with bronze or red-green iridescence; ischium etched in red with purple stripe; merus red, yellow and white with purplish spines; carpus red and purple; propodus with stripes of purple, dark red and light with some fine yellow spots; dactyl violet, red and white; claw pale yellow. Eyestalk brown; cornea black with a film of white and red chromatophores. Antennal flagellum yellowish.

Habitat—Mud and sand. Inhabit small shells which barely cover the small abdomen and often are covered with hydractinia. An active species.

Size—Shield length: male 18 mm.

Range—Sea of Japan, Arctic Ocean, Chukchi and Bering seas, and Alaska to Puget Sound, Washington; from 16 to 412 m.

Distribution in British Columbia—Widespread but not abundant.

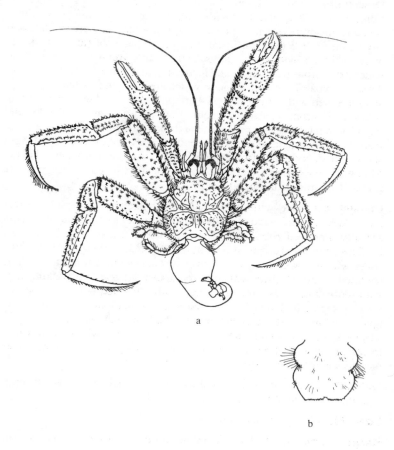

a

b

Fig. 39 *Labidochirus splendescens*: a, male, dorsal view; b, telson.

115

Orthopagurus minimus (Holmes 1900)*

Pagurus minimus, Pylopagurus minimus

Description—Shield slightly longer than wide and with a distinct rostrum. Eyestalk long and stout with slightly dilated cornea. Right cheliped subequal in length to walking legs and sparsely setose; merus with few, if any, spines but 2 teeth on distal margin; carpus subequal in width to merus, with a row of spines and scattered spiny granules dorsally; hand wider than carpus proximally and increasing in width distally, with spines dorsally on palm and both fingers, which are wide and flattened dorsally and margined with a tight row of sharp pointed curved teeth and cutting edges with strong calcareous teeth. Left cheliped small, slender and setose with few spines or granules; hand convex without serrate margins. Walking legs slender, setose with propodus and dactyl subequal in length and width; dactyl with strong spines ventrally and a sharp, curved claw. Abdomen straight with calcified plates dorsally; pleopods only on left side and symmetrical uropods and telson.

Colour—Carapace with shield reddish orange; rostrum pink, lateral areas dark red and wine-red. Abdomen straw-coloured with red spots dorsally; light red laterally. Tail fan red. Right cheliped with dark red ischium; merus and carpus straw-coloured with dark red spines and teeth. Hand wine-red with yellowish finger tips and white cutting teeth. Left cheliped straw-coloured with fine red spots. 1st and 2nd walking legs with red ischium; rest straw-coloured with a few red dots. 3rd and 4th walking legs red. Eyestalk wine-red and straw-coloured with irregular opaque white bands; cornea semicircular with curved bands of pale yellow and black. Antennule red and straw-coloured with opaque white bands. Antenna with red and white base; the rest straw-coloured. Small individuals often straw-coloured with little or no red.

Habitat—Usually inhabit Dentalium shells which they actively drag over the substrate of broken shell and gravel.

Size—Shield length: male 5.6 mm.

Range—Tartar Strait, East Sakhalin (northwest Pacific), and British Columbia to San Diego; from 11 to 64 m.

Distribution in British Columbia—Widespread but rarely collected.

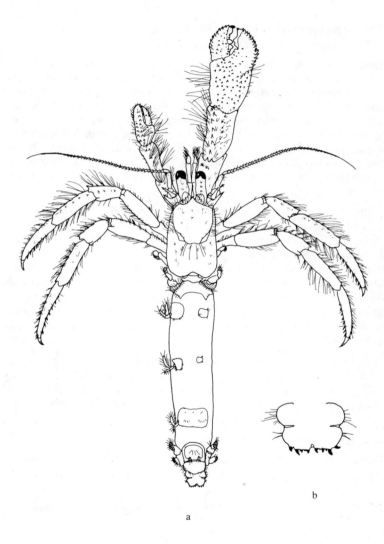

b

a

Fig. 40 *Orthopagurus minimus*: a, male, dorsal view; b, telson.

117

Discorsopagurus schmitti (Stevens 1925)
Pylopagurus schmitti, Orthopagurus schmitti

Description—Carapace: shield slightly longer than wide. Eyestalk relatively long and stout; cornea a little dilated. Right cheliped setose and slightly longer than walking legs, with spines and granules scattered over surface, especially on carpus and hand; with inner margin of palm serrate with large, sharp teeth and outer margin with a row of spines. Left cheliped more slender but nearly as long as right; carpus and hand with spines and sharp granules. Walking legs slender and setose; dactyl shorter than propodus; claw curved and stout. Abdomen straight; uropods symmetrical; pleopods only on left side. Calcified plates indicate segmentation of abdomen.

Colour—Carapace: shield light brown and posterior brown with mottling of purplish red and grey. Chelipeds yellow with red-brown dappling; fingers dark brown laterally and scarlet and white dorsally. Walking legs: ischium red-brown; merus yellowish with proximal and distal bands of dappled red-brown, carpus yellow with red-brown dappling dorsally; propodus yellowish with narrow red-brown band proximally; dactyl with bands of red-brown, yellow and scarlet; claw yellow. Eyestalk greenish-brown proximally and blue-grey with red stripes distally; cornea black with some gold flecks. Antennal flagellum orange or scarlet and somewhat translucent.

Habitat—Usually occupies empty, encrusted, leathery tubes of the worm *Sabellaria cementatium*, in deep water, or empty calcareous tubes of *Serpula vermicularis*, in shallow water. Because these tubes are encrusting forms, the crabs are mostly sessile, but quite mobile when inhabiting a loose portion of tube.

Size—Shield length: male 4.5 mm.

Range—Northwestern Pacific; Hayward Strait, Sitka Sound, Alaska (57°20'15"N, 135°50'30"W), to Puget Sound, Washington; intertidal to 220 m.

Distribution in British Columbia—Widespread but easily missed.

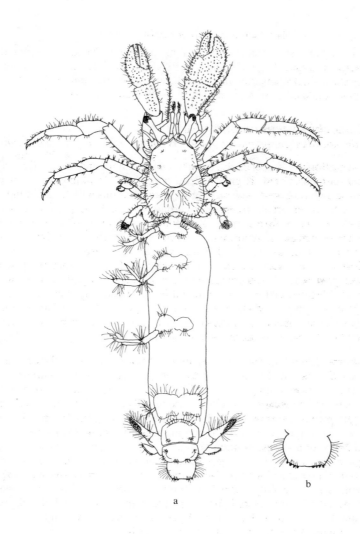

Fig. 41 *Discorsopagurus schmitti*: a, female, dorsal view; b, telson.

The Genus *Elassochirus* Benedict 1892

Carapace: shield calcified, rest membranous. Maxillipeds widely separated at base. Right cheliped much larger than left. Eyescale subrectangular with deep median furrow. 4th pereiopod (3rd walking leg) dactyl with specialized type A, P_4 structure (McLaughlin 1974).

Elassochirus tenuimanus (Dana 1851)

Bernhardus tenuimanus, Eupagurus tenuimanus, Pagurus tenuimanus

Description—Carapace: shield subequal in length and width. Eyestalk stout; cornea dilated. Right cheliped longer than walking legs; surface with numerous granules of varying sizes and margins with larger granules or teeth; merus short, triangular; carpus wide and slightly convex and palm even wider than carpus, with compressed dorso-ventral area with the upper margin of palm making a curved protruberance; fixed finger short and wide at base and finger longer and narrower with strong calcareous teeth. Left cheliped slender and much smaller than right, with fewer granules and teeth; hand with dorsal surface slightly convex with elevated beaded margins on palm and fixed finger; finger with a cutting edge of a tight row of short, stout corneous setae. 1st and 2nd walking legs short and stout, with dorsal ridge of carpus and propodus serrate; dactyl with corneous spines and a stout claw.

Colour—Shield marbled with white and brown, the rest of the carapace with red, white and yellow. Right cheliped: ischium white with orange patches; merus with orange and greenish brown and 2 cobalt-blue patches, and an orange and yellow band distally and white marginal teeth; carpus greenish brown with white, orange-ringed, granules; hand light brown with light red streaks and white teeth. Left cheliped similar. 1st and 2nd walking legs: ischium orange and yellow; merus yellow with an orange streak dorsally, a large, cobalt-blue patch on each face, orange distally with red and white spines; carpus with 3 dark red stripes dorsally, a white stripe medially and yellow ventrally; propodus with 2 red stripes composed of a row of red spots, opaque white patch medially; dactyl cream with rows of dark red spots. Eyestalk; orange brown bands; cornea grey-green. Antennal flagellum orange to red-brown.

Habitat—Mud, sand, gravel, shell or mixture of these.

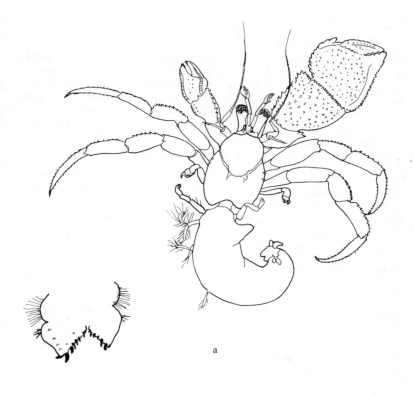

a

b

Fig. 42 *Elassochirus tenuimanus*: a, female, dorsal view; b, telson.

Size—Shield length: male 23.4 mm.

Range—Northwestern Pacific Ocean, Aleutian Islands, Alaska, to Puget Sound, Washington; intertidal to 388 m.

Distribution in British Columbia—Common in suitable habitat.

Elassochirus cavimanus (Miers 1879)

Eupagurus cavimanus, Pagurus cavimanus, Pagurus munitus

Description—Carapace: surface smooth, shield subequal in length and width. Eyestalk stout; cornea slightly inflated. Right cheliped subequal in length to walking legs and most surfaces smooth; merus short, triangular, with a few sharp granules near distal denticulate margin; carpus convex medially and produced laterally into flat "wings" on either side, inner and distal margins denticulate and a scattered row of small spines mid-dorsally; hand subrectangular with wide fingers; left hand oval with wide fixed finger. Walking legs compressed and slightly setose.

Colour—Carapace orange or scarlet. Right cheliped: merus and carpus violet with orange margins; hand pale orange or flesh coloured and violet; teeth white. Left cheliped similar except more violet on hand. Walking legs deep red or orange with distinct white polka dots, claw brown. Eyestalk orange; cornea black with yellow rings. Antennal flagellum translucent with a tinge of orange.

Habitat—Mud or sandy bottom.

Size—Shield length: male 21.1 mm.

Range—Japan and northwestern Pacific from the Bering Sea to Departure Bay, British Columbia, and Cobb Seamount (46°44'N, 130°47'W), off Washington; from 36 to 252 m.

Distribution in British Columbia—Only a few scattered records, mostly in the north.

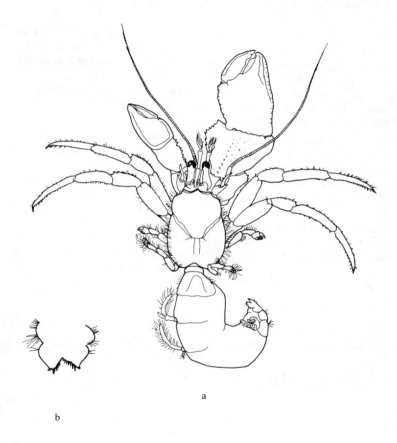

a

b

Fig. 43   *Elassochirus cavimanus*: a, male, dorsal view; b, telson.

Elassochirus gilli (Benedict 1892)*
Eupagurus gilli, Pagurus gilli

Description—Carapace: surface smooth; shield subequal in length and width. Eyestalk stout; cornea not inflated. Right cheliped surface smooth, subequal in length to walking legs; merus short and triangular, distal margin denticulate; carpus convex and produced laterally into flat "wings", inner and distal margin serrate; hand with lateral margins parallel and fingers wide at base; left hand oval and fixed finger wide. Walking legs compressed and slightly setose.

Colour—Carapace: shield grey and brown with light anterior margin and pale yellow median stripe; posterior part brown and maroon with grey and cream stripes and dots. Abdomen maroon and cream. Right cheliped: ischium white and scarlet; merus scarlet with white dots distally; carpus scarlet and orange dorsally, and ventrally; hand orange with brown fingers bordered in white; teeth white, ventrally yellow. Left cheliped scarlet and orange only. Walking legs scarlet and orange with white spots at junctions of merus and propodus and rows of small white dots on lateral faces of propodus and dactylus; claw brown. Eyestalk red and brown with distal margins white; cornea black with gold flecks. Antennal flagellum scarlet.

Habitat—Rocky areas.

Size—Shield length: male 20.4 m.

Range—Northwestern Pacific Ocean, Bering Sea, Alaska, to Puget Sound, Washington; intertidal to 200 m.

Distribution in British Columbia—Fairly common in suitable habitat.

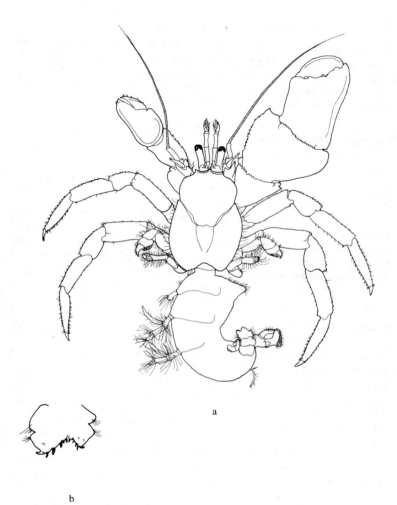

a

b

Fig. 44 *Elassochirus gilli*: a, female, dorsal view; b, telson.

125

The Genus *Pagurus* Fabricius 1775

Hermit crabs with anterior carapace (shield) calcified and posterior mainly membranous. Third maxillipeds widely separated at base. Right cheliped larger than left. No paired pleopods on well-developed abdomen: pleopods on left side only. Uropods asymmetrical and adapted, with telson, to anchor animal within shell or other habitat.

Pagurus armatus (Dana 1851)
Bernhardus armatus, Eupagurus armatus, Eupagurus ochotensis, Pagurus ochotensis

Description—Carapace: shield broader than long. Eyestalk relatively short and stout; cornea dilated and ovate. Right cheliped stout, shorter than walking legs; carpus and hand covered with sharp spines which are larger on margins and less dense on ventral surfaces. Left cheliped similar, but slender. 1st and 2nd walking legs stout; merus compressed laterally, with spines and denticulated ridges; carpus and propodus with dorsal margins and serrate and small spines on faces; dactyl longer than merus and twisted with upper margin serrated and ridged and lower margin with close-set corneous spines; claw sharp and stout.

Colour—Carapace: shield with areas of white, brown, and shell pink laterally; posterior red, apricot and white. Chelipeds: ischium with brown bands: merus pink, brown and white with an orange band distally and margins and teeth dark brown; carpus light brown, yellow, white and blue areas with dark brown spines; palm pale yellow with dark brown spines medially and red marginally with fingers white or grey-blue with white tips and teeth. 1st and 2nd walking legs have ischium yellow and white; merus opaque white, tan, orange and mahogany with scattered dark brown spots; carpus yellow with dark spines, a narrow mahogany stripe on median posterior face and a white patch distally; propodus white, yellow, orange and a brown area with a mahogany stripe ventrally; dactyl white, orange and violet-blue with dark spines and 2 narrow brown stripes; claw yellow. Green or gold iridescence on surfaces of appendages. Eyestalk with red band at base, and opaque white and brown bands; cornea black. Antennal flagellum pale yellow.

Habitat—Sand, mud, shell or gravel.

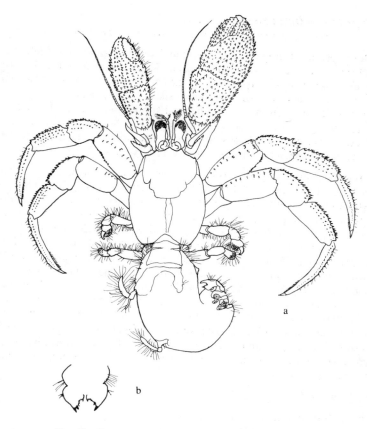

Fig. 45 *Pagurus armatus*: a, male, dorsal view; b, telson.

Size—Shield length: male 19.6 mm.

Range—Unalaska, Alaska, to San Diego, California; intertidal to 146 m.

Distribution in British Columbia—Common in dredged material. May be taken intertidally in some areas during low night tides in winter.

Pagurus ochotensis Brandt 1851

Eupagurus ochotensis, Eupagurus alaskensis, Pagurus alaskensis

Description—Carapace: shield broader than long. Eyestalk relatively short and stout; cornea dilated and ovate. Right cheliped stout and shorter than walking legs; carpus with spines mid-dorsally in two rows and marginally; hand with small spines or sharp granules and stronger spines marginally and ventrally. Left cheliped similar but smaller. 1st and 2nd walking legs stout; carpus and propodus with serrate dorsal margins; dactyl long, broad and twisted with serrate dorsal margins, 2 shallow sulci, and close-set corneous spines ventrally; claw sharp and stout.

Colour—Carapace: shield pink and maroon; lateral opaque yellow and posterior pink and scarlet marbled with maroon spots. Right cheliped with ischium white; merus white with pearly iridescence and maroon streaks and a terminal band; carpus grey or brown with dark grey spines, pink, green and bronze iridescence; hand white or flesh coloured with grey and brown spines and granules, a maroon streak from inner distal margin to near tip of fixed finger, and finger also with a maroon streak on cutting margin. Left cheliped similar but no prominent maroon streaks on hand. 1st and 2nd walking legs: ischium yellowish; merus gold, maroon and blue areas and green iridescence; carpus and propodus similar but with two maroon stripes in addition; dactyl with anterior face maroon, with wide blue stripes and posterior face with pale blue stripes. Eyestalk white with red spots and greenish yellow band distally; cornea black and greenish yellow. Antennal flagellum pinkish brown. Depth of colour varies with individuals.

Habitat—Mud or sand bottom.

Size—Shield length: male 27.7 mm.

Range—Northwestern Pacific and Pribilof Islands, Alaska, to off Point Arena, California; intertidal to 388 m.

Distribution in British Columbia—Common.

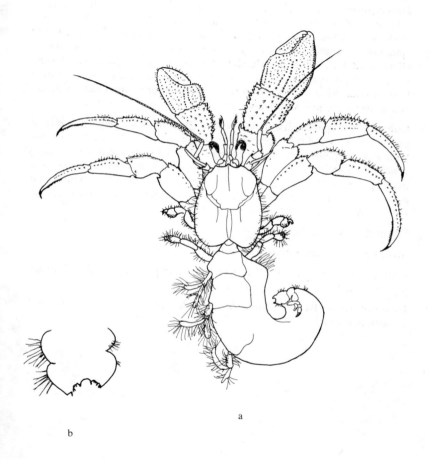

a

b

Fig. 46 *Pagurus ochotensis*: a, male, dorsal view; b, telson.

129

Pagurus aleuticus (Benedict 1892)

Eupagurus aleuticus

Description—Carapace: shield subequal in length and width. Eyestalks relatively short and stout, with cornea dilated and ovate. Right cheliped stout, shorter than walking legs and with carpus and hand covered with spines and granules, outer margins serrate. Most of the spines are bifid (2 sharp points). Left cheliped slender. 1st and 2nd walking legs with serrate margins and dorsal rows of spines; dactyl long, stout and twisted with a longitudinal sulcus and with a row of close-set corneous spines ventrally and terminating in a stout claw.

Colour—Carapace: shield red or brown with paler network; lateral yellowish with red dots; posterior red and yellow. Abdomen pink and yellow. Chelipeds pink, red or orange with red spines and some iridescence. 1st and 2nd walking legs iridescent pink with maroon streaks and dark spines; dactyl orange with a red stripe on outer face and dorsal groove dark red. Eyestalk white and tan; cornea black and greenish yellow. Antennal flagellum orange or tan.

Habitat—Mud and/or sand bottom.

Size—Shield length: male 28.1 mm.

Range—Northwestern Pacific from the Bering Sea to Eureka, California, (40°41′N, 127°31.7′W); from 15 to 435 m.

Distribution in British Columbia—Widespread in suitable areas and usually below 70 m.

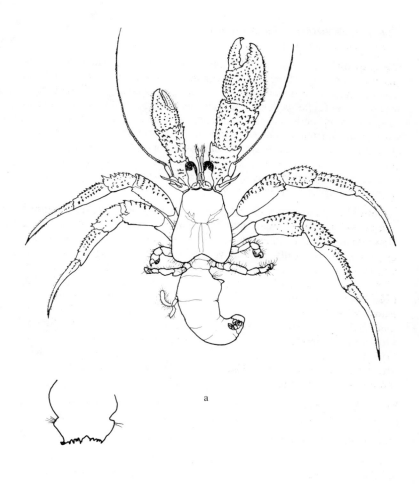

a

b

Fig. 47 *Pagurus aleuticus*: a, male, dorsal view; b, telson.

131

Pagurus samuelis (Stimpson 1857)*
Eupagurus samuelis

Description—Carapace: shield longer than broad. Eyestalk stout; cornea not dilated. Right cheliped shorter than walking legs; carpus and hand with numerous granules and lateral margins beaded; outline of hand semi-oval. Left cheliped smaller than right with ventral margin of merus cut into strong teeth. 1st and 2nd walking legs stout and setose; dactyl slightly shorter than propodus and with stout movable spines ventrally; claw strong and curved. Propodus and dactyl of left 2nd walking leg (3rd pereiopod) with spines and granules ventrally. This is also found in several other intertidal species and the function does not seem to be known. It may be useful for gripping rock faces.

Colour—Carapace mottled blue, brown and green or black with 5 opaque white stripes, the central 3 running from the rostrum to the posterior margin, the other 2 postero-laterally. Right cheliped with ischium olive green dorsally and blue ventrally; merus and carpus olive green with red granules; palm greenish brown with red and white-tipped granules; fingers blue to white with orange tips. Left cheliped similar but more orange on finger tips. 1st and 2nd walking legs olive green to brownish green with dark red striae and an irregular china blue band margined with a narrow red brown band; dactyl china blue with a thin red mid-lateral stripe on both faces and, on dorsal ridge, a patch of orange and of white terminally; claw dark. Eyestalk red brown and olive green with white band distally; cornea black with white flecks forming concentric circles. Antennal flagellum translucent red.

Habitat—High intertidal, often inhabiting black turban shells (*Tegula funebralis*) and sharing the same habitat as the living gastropods.

Size—Shield length: male 8 mm.

Range—Nootka Sound (49°45′N, 126°50′W), British Columbia, to northwest Baja California, Mexico; high intertidal. Not Japan.

Distribution in British Columbia—Known only from Nootka Sound to Port Renfrew.

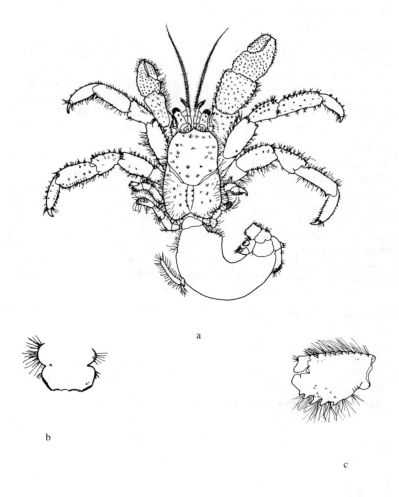

Fig. 48 *Pagurus samuelis*: a, male, dorsal view; b, telson; c, merus of right cheliped, lateral view.

Pagurus hemphilli (Benedict 1892)*
Eupagurus hemphilli

Description—Carapace: shield distinctly longer than wide. Eyestalk long and slender, cornea slightly dilated. Right cheliped much larger than left, finely granulate with some teeth on distal margins of merus and carpus; carpus laterally compressed and inflated ventrally; hand, oval with a beading of granules on the margins; left hand much smaller than right and laterally compressed. 1st and 2nd walking legs subequal in length to right cheliped, stout and serrate on dorsal margins of carpus and propodus.

Colour—Carapace: shield greenish brown; rest purple and blue with white dots. Abdomen pale purple, blue, pink and white. Right cheliped red and dark purple-red; hand dark greenish brown with pale blue granules; fingers red with blue granules; tips of fingers yellow and teeth white. Left cheliped similar but hand red and finger tips scarlet and yellow. Walking legs dark red with blue-white granules, distal half of dactyl orange and scarlet with dark brown claw. Eyestalk brown to cream; cornea black with gold semicircles. Antennal flagellum scarlet. Juveniles without the deep red colour and walking legs white with varying amounts of red proximally but dactyls have orange tips.

Habitat—Low intertidal and subtidal on open coast among seaweed covered rocks.

Size—Shield length: male 9.8 mm.

Range—Klokachef Island (57°25'N, 135°52'W), Alaska, to south of San Miguel Island, California (34°01'N, 120°24'W); intertidal to 50 m.

Distribution in British Columbia—Only on open coasts.

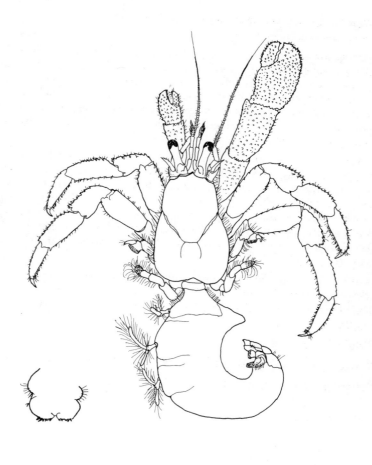

a

b

Fig. 49 *Pagurus hemphilli*: a, female, dorsal view; b, telson.

135

Pagurus granosimanus (Stimpson 1858)

Eupagurus granosimanus

Description—Carapace: shield slightly longer than broad. Eyestalk relatively long; cornea slightly dilated. Chelipeds stout; merus with small granules, spines and tufts of short setae; carpus and hand subequal in length with numerous flat-topped granules on both dorsal and ventral surfaces. 1st and 2nd walking legs stout, about equal in length to right cheliped and with scattered granules and short setae; dactyl slightly longer than propodus.

Colour—Carapace: shield white with brown and green marbling; sides of carapace reddish brown with blue dots; posterior kelp brown with longitudinal rows of cream dots. Chelipeds kelp brown with pale blue granules, some of which have white tips. 1st and 2nd walking legs kelp brown, darkest dorsally, with pale blue granules; tip of dactyl red brown, claw greenish brown. Eyestalk dark kelp brown; eyescale edged with cream; cornea black with silver flecks. Antennal flagellum translucent tan to red.

Habitat—Intertidal in rocky and gravelled areas. Often congregate in tide pools where they tolerate fairly high water temperatures. Usually inhabit large heavy shells, such as *Thais*, into which the animal can withdraw completely.

Size—Shield length: male 9.6 mm.

Range—Unalaska, Alaska, to Ensenada, Mexico; intertidal to 36 m.

Distribution in British Columbia—Common intertidally.

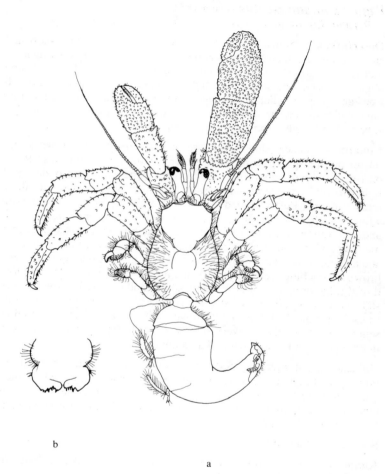

b

a

Fig. 50 *Pagurus granosimanus*: a, male, dorsal view; b, telson.

137

Pagurus hirsutiusculus (Dana 1851)

Bernhardus hirsutiusculus, Eupagurus hirsutiusculus

Description—Carapace: shield broader than long. Eyestalk short and stout; cornea not dilated. Right cheliped stout, shorter than walking legs; merus and carpus setose and with granules, spines and striae; hand slightly convex, sparsely setose and with many small granules. Proportions and shape of cheliped changes with growth. Left cheliped similar but smaller than right. 1st and 2nd walking legs setose; dactyl slender, subequal in length to propodus; claw curved.

Colour—Carapace: shield dark brown masked by light brown setae; posterior grey-green with dark brown streaks and striations. Right cheliped: ischium light brown, merus dirty white with striae of dark and light brown; carpus greenish brown, hand light grey-brown with dirty white fingers. Left cheliped brown, blue-grey, greenish-brown with white band distally on merus; hand red-brown with tan or orange tips. 1st and 2nd walking legs: ischium light brown or bluish; merus dark brown medially, white and/or blue; carpus light brown with dark brown streaks and a distal white patch with narrow red margin; dactyl greenish or red-brown with a blue area proximally and a red stripe on each lateral face, dorsal ridge brown; ventral movable spines and claw dark brown. Eyestalk grey with dark brown streaks; cornea black with concentric gold rings. Antennal flagellum kelp brown with a gold dot on every other segment, proximally, to every 6th, distally. Juveniles with much less intense colour and more white than adults.

Habitat—High intertidal. Small individuals occur in great numbers in upper zone tidepools, despite high temperature and salinity, where they hide among tufts of calcareous algae. All stages very agile and have a tendency to use small light shells which are readily abandoned when in full flight from predators.

Size—Shield length: male 9.8 mm.

Range—Northwestern Pacific and Pribilof Islands, Alaska, to southern California; intertidal to 110 m.

Distribution in British Columbia—Ubiquitous intertidally

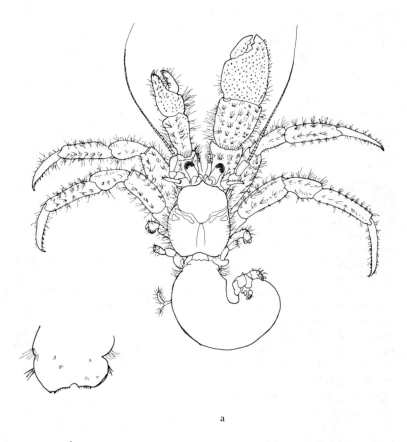

a

b

Fig. 51 *Pagurus hirsutiusculus*: a, male, dorsal view; b, telson.

Pagurus beringanus (Benedict 1892)*

Eupagurus beringanus, E. newcombei, Pagurus newcombei

Description—Carapace: shield subequal in length and width. Eyestalk long and slender. Right cheliped long and stout, slightly shorter than walking legs; merus with upper surface convex, some linear striations, large distal marginal teeth dorsally and 2 large knobs ventrally; carpus long, convex with rows of large granules and spines; hand convex with ridges and many granules, spines and serrate margins. Left cheliped much smaller. 1st and 2nd walking legs stout and setose; merus laterally compressed.

Colour—Carapace: shield pale grey with marbling of dark grey, red, yellow and tan with red dots and front margins scarlet; posterior carapace and abdomen marbled with grey, brown and purple, red and white dots. Chelipeds: ischium white and orange; merus greenish brown, with red striae and a scarlet band on distal margin, ventrally white, blue and yellow with orange knobs; carpus greenish-brown with orange spines and tubercles; hand greenish-brown fading to white on fingers, sharp granules with white tips, scarlet at base and tips of fingers with corneous tips brown and teeth white. 1st and 2nd walking legs: ischium grey with red and opaque white patches; merus pale greenish brown with red spots and distal bands of red and scarlet; carpus and propodus grey green to white with dark red spots, scarlet patch terminally on propodus; dactyl with 2 dark red bands separated by white, with red dots; claw dark. Eyestalk greenish-brown; cornea black with gold semicircles. Antennal flagellum translucent with red laterally. Juveniles and small individuals not as highly coloured as adults with white, pale green, and grey and orange granules and red or yellow bands on merus of chelipeds and on propodus of walking legs.

Habitat—In rocky areas intertidally where water is cold and, subtidally, where temperatures are higher. Prefers a large, heavy shell within which the animal can withdraw completely. Tends to congregate in large numbers in shaded rock crevices at low tide.

Size—Shield length: male 15.5 mm.

Range—Bering Sea and Aleutian Islands, Alaska, to Monterey, California; intertidal to 364 m.

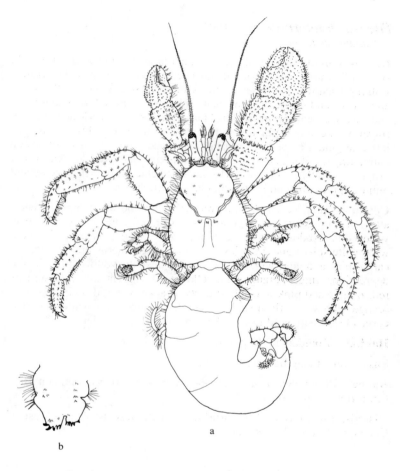

b

a

Fig. 52 *Pagurus beringanus*: a, male, dorsal view; b, telson.

Distribution in British Columbia—Common intertidally in cold-water areas such as the Juan de Fuca Strait, but not so in the warmer waters of the Strait of Georgia.

Pagurus tanneri (Benedict 1892)
Eupagurus tanneri

Description—Carapace: shield subequal in length and width. Eyestalk short and stout; cornea dilated. Right cheliped stout, slightly shorter than walking legs; merus setose; carpus with small spines on dorsal surface and serrate and setose margins; hand spiny with a raised triangular ridge and base less than half the width of the palm; apex reaches level of base of finger. Left cheliped smaller and slender, with hand slightly swollen on left side, and a curved raised ridge margined with 2 rows of spines on palm; fingers elongate. 1st and 2nd walking legs slender; carpi and propodi dorsally serrate; dactyl with stiff setae on dorsal margins and minute spines on ventral margin; claw small, sharp.

Colour—Carapace: shield red, orange, yellow and white dappled; laterally red with white reticulations; posterior red and orange with pale yellow dots. Abdomen with red, pink, orange and white areas. Chelipeds with white spines and granules; ischium orange; merus pink to orange; carpus pink to orange with some yellow striae; palm yellowish, with pink depressions; fingers orange with yellow teeth. 1st and 2nd walking legs red, orange and pink in patches; dactyl orange with red setae. Eyestalk orange with white tip distally; eyescales orange with white margins; cornea black with gold flecks. Antennal flagellum scarlet.

Habitat—Boulders in deep water

Size—Shield length: male 18.1 mm.

Range—Bering Sea and Unalaska, Alaska to off San Simeon Bay, California; 91 to 1372 m.

Distribution in British Columbia—La Perouse Bank and west of Clayoquot Sound, Vancouver Island.

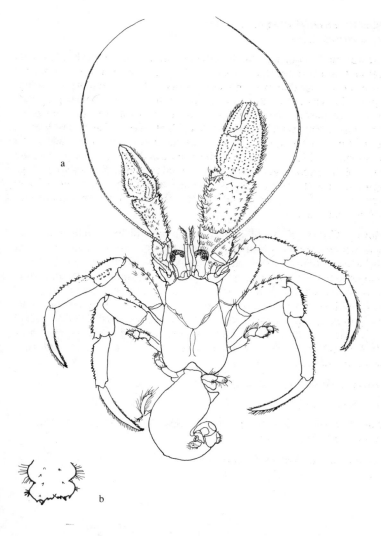

Fig. 53 *Pagurus tanneri*: a, male, dorsal view; b, telson.

143

Pagurus cornutus (Benedict 1892)
Eupagurus cornutus

Description—Carapace: shield subequal in length and width. Eyestalk short and stout; cornea distinctly dilated. Right cheliped stout, somewhat setose and shorter than walking legs; merus with toothed margin distally; carpus with serrate margins and a few spines dorsally; hand granulate with serrate margins, a few spines on dorsal surface and a large triangular, horn-shaped ridge with base about ½ width of palm and apex past level of base of finger. Left cheliped stout, with hand swollen on left side and a narrow spined ridge running from the middle of the base of the palm to the middle of the fixed finger which has a curved tip. 1st and 2nd walking legs setose, stout with serrate margins on carpi of 1st legs and right 2nd leg; dactyls with stiff setae on dorsal margins and movable spines on ventral margins; claw sharp.

Colour—Carapace: shield orange and pink with pale yellow median streak which continues to mid-posterior part of carapace; rest red with some white patches. Abdomen pink and yellow. Chelipeds: ischium red: merus orange with cream striae and spines, white marginal teeth; carpus red to orange with yellow spines; palm orange medially and pink marginally with yellow spines; fingers pink with yellow tips and white teeth. Walking legs deep and pale red; merus with pink band distally; dactyl mostly pale; claw translucent. Eyestalk orange with light spots; eyescales orange with pale borders; cornea black with silver "stars". Antennal flagellum pale translucent orange.

Habitat—Mud or sand in deep water.

Size—Shield length: male 18.7 mm.

Range—Northwestern Pacific and Bering Sea to Oregon (46°02'N, 124°43.7'W); 160 to 830 m.

Distribution in British Columbia—Queen Charlotte Sound, Dixon Entrance and off Barkley Sound.

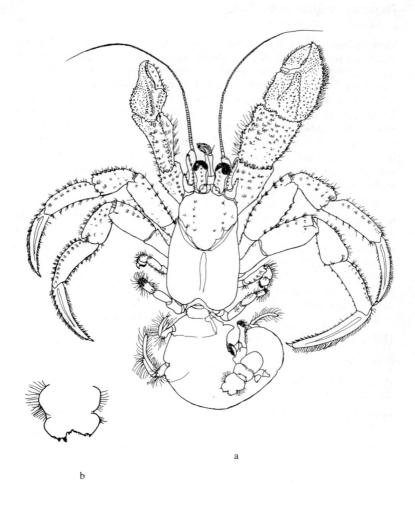

a

b

Fig. 54   *Pagurus cornutus*: a, female, dorsal view; b, telson.

145

Pagurus confragosus (Benedict 1892)
Eupagurus confragosus

Description—Carapace: shield subequal in length and width. Eyestalk short and stout; cornea dilated. Right cheliped stout, setose and shorter than walking legs; merus setose; carpus with small spines on dorsal surface and with serrate margins; hand spined and with a raised triangular ridge whose base is about ⅔ width of palm and apex past level of base of finger. Left cheliped slender with rows of spines on carpus; hand with palm greatly inflated on outer side of a convex ridge and with a row of large spines on right side and small ones on left, extending from base of hand nearly to middle of fingers. 1st and 2nd walking legs stout; carpi serrate marginly on 1st legs; dactyls with stiff setae on dorsal margin, and small movable spines ventrally; claws small.

Colour—Carapace white with pink and red mottling. Abdomen cream and white with red mottling. Chelipeds red and white blotched proximally; carpus white with bright red splotches and spines; hand pink and fingers with white cutting surfaces. Walking legs with ischium pink, red and white; merus and carpus red, white and pale tan; propodus with bright red bands proximally and distally and with lighter colour between; dactyl red with a fine lateral stripe proximally, pink medially and orange distally. Eyestalk pink with white stripe and red patches; cornea black with gold flecks. Depth of colour varies in individuals.

Habitat—Rocky, mud, sand or gravel.

Size—Shield length: male 20.2 mm.

Range—Bristol Bay, Alaska, to Columbia River mouth, Oregon; 55 to 435 m.

Distribution in British Columbia—Not common but widespread.

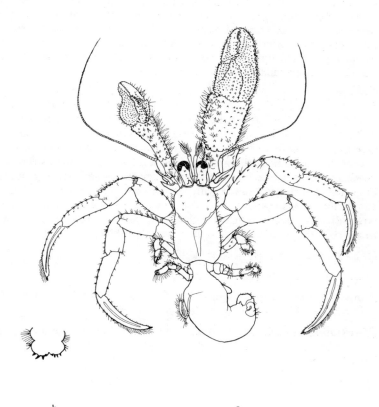

b   a

Fig. 55   *Pagurus confragosus*: a, male, dorsal view; b, telson.

Pagurus sp.

Description—Carapace: shield longer than wide. Eyestalk long; cornea not dilated; eyescales with 1 to 3 sharp-pointed marginal teeth. Right cheliped shorter than walking legs with rows of stout spines on dorsal surface of palm and fingers and serrate margins; carpus with inner margin serrate and smaller spines dorsally; merus with ventral margin serrate. Left cheliped shorter and more slender than right and fingers proportionately longer; similarly spined. Walking legs long and no serrate margins. All appendages with scattered tufts of setae.

Colour—Brilliant. Shield orange and scarlet, dark red, and white spots; rest of carapace reticulated dark red with rows of small white dots. Abdomen yellow or red with blue tinges. Both chelipeds have merus and carpus dark red with patches of intense violet margined with crimson on both faces; palm orange with dark red network and white spots; fingers orange. 1st and 2nd walking legs: merus reddish orange with stripes of violet or bluish white margined with crimson on both faces; carpus, propodus and dactyl orange with similar bluish white stripes. These stripes do not completely fade when preserved and are useful diagnostically. Eyestalk translucent with scarlet bands and patches and white bases. Antennules with bands of red, white and blue.

Habitat—Sand or gravel and broken shell.

Size—Shield length: male 3.3 mm.

Range—Queen Charlotte Sound (51°45'N, 128°05'W), British Columbia, to border of California and Mexico; 6 to 109 m.

Distribution in British Columbia—Queen Charlotte Sound and outer coast of Vancouver Island south to Barkley Sound.

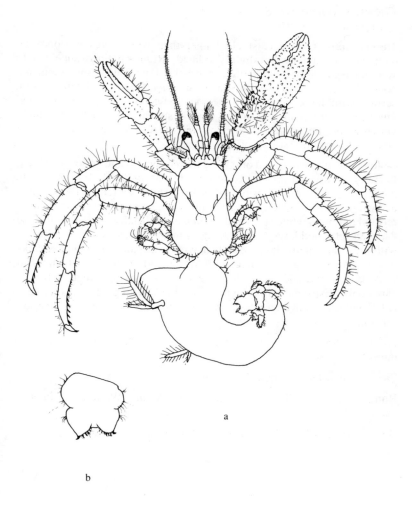

a

b

Fig. 56 *Pagurus* sp.: a, male, dorsal view; b, telson.

Pagurus kennerlyi (Stimpson 1864)
Eupagurus kennerlyi

Description—Carapace: shield longer than wide. Eyestalk long and slender; cornea may be slightly dilated. Right cheliped subequal to walking legs, setose, with tufts of bristles longer than spines but not concealing them; carpus with spines on surface but inner lateral margin serrate with large corneous-tipped teeth which increase in size and number distally; palm and fingers heavily spined. Left cheliped smaller, with rows of stout spines. 1st and 2nd walking legs setose, relatively short and stout; carpi of 1st pair of legs serrate.

Colour—Carapace: shield orange, dark red, brown and yellow marbled, laterally brown and cream, posteriorly bright and dark red, and white with yellow dots at base of tufts of setae. Abdomen red, yellow, brown and white marbled. Chelipeds: ischium tan and white; merus dark to light red and tan, with white spots and a white band distally; carpus with some dark red setae and large blue or white spines with dark corneous tips, or with a red band; palm dark red and tan with large pale blue or white, dark-tipped spines; fingers orange with white cutting teeth. 1st and 2nd walking legs red and tan with white patches forming irregular bands; claws dark. Eyestalk kelp brown; cornea black with gold flecks. Antennal flagellum with alternate uneven bands of dark brown or maroon separated by narrower translucent bands.

Habitat—Rarely intertidal; subtidal on rocky areas, gravel, sand or mud.

Size—Shield length: male 19.2 mm.

Range—Aleutian Islands, Alaska, to Puget Sound, Washington; intertidal to 274 m.

Distribution in British Columbia—Widely distributed.

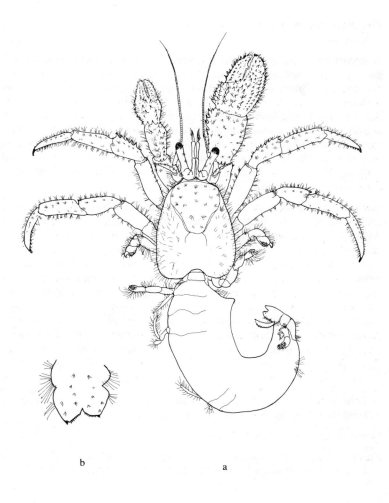

b   a

Fig. 57   *Pagurus kennerlyi*: a, male, dorsal view; b, telson.

151

Pagurus caurinus Hart 1971*
Pagurus setosus

Description—Carapace: shield subequal in length and width; lateral areas covered with long soft setae. Eyestalk long, slender and medially constricted; cornea slightly dilated. Right cheliped nearly as long as walking legs, setose, with tufts of long setae; merus with small granules dorsally and 1 or 2 knobs ventrally; carpus slightly convex dorsally and armed with small spines and a serrate inner margin; hand longer than subequal merus and carpus, with about 7 rows of sharp spines and serrated margins. Left cheliped smaller but similar to right. 1st and 2nd walking legs stout and setose, only 1st right leg with dorsal margin of carpus serrate; claw stout and curved.

Colour—Carapace light grey and cream with longitudinal purple stripes, each with a row of light dots, and laterally marbled with red-brown. Abdomen purple and grey. Chelipeds each with merus brown and grey and a dull white or yellowish distal band; carpus grey-green and red-brown with spines grey-based and orange-tipped; hand light greenish-brown and grey; spines orange-tipped and finger tips orange-red. 1st and 2nd walking legs: merus red-brown with an irregular yellowish-white band margined distally with orange; carpus brown with grey spots and inner face yellowish; propodus with narrow white band, a wide red-brown band, a grey spotted band and an opaque white band; dactyl red-brown with grey spots becoming orange near tip; claw translucent brown. Eyestalk light with greenish brown bands; cornea black and yellow. Antennal flagellum orange. Colour somewhat masked by long, tan setae.

Habitat—Intertidal in cold water on outer coast but rarely so in warmer waters. Rocky areas, and sand, mud or gravel.

Size—Shield length: male 7 mm.

Range—South of Comfort Cove, Port Gravina (60°43'N, 146°7'W), Alaska, to Los Angeles breakwater, San Pedro, California; intertidal to 126 m.

Distribution in British Columbia—Common but probably overlooked because of small size.

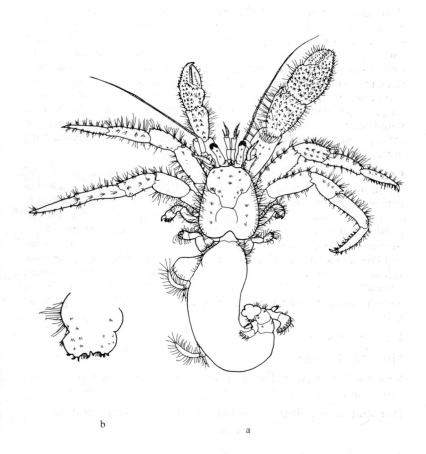

b

a

Fig. 58 *Pagurus caurinus*: a, male, dorsal view; b, telson.

Pagurus capillatus (Benedict 1892)
Eupagurus capillatus, Pagurus setosus

Description—Carapace: shield nearly as broad as long. Eyestalk slender and long; cornea slightly dilated. Surface spines on chelipeds are hidden by a dense covering of long, soft plumose setae; merus with a few small spines and tufts of long setae, distal margin with numerous small teeth; carpus setose with inner margin serrated with larger spines than those scattered over dorsal surface and outer margin; palm and fingers with setae covering many rows of spines. Hand of adult male proportionately longer than that of female. Left cheliped relatively small and slender with long fingers. 1st and 2nd walking legs slender and setose, with carpi, of 1st legs only, serrate on dorsal margins; dactyl long and slender, with minute movable spines on ventral margin; claw stout.

Colour—Carapace: shield cream with mottled red, brown, green, and cream mid-dorsally and laterally; posterior pink and brown. Abdomen pale pink with brown spots. Chelipeds: merus white with irregular bands of rose and brown; carpus white with apricot spines, brown and red mottled; hand light brown and fingers with apricot tips. Walking legs: ischium pink, red and yellow splotched; merus irregularly banded in red and brown; carpus and propodus each with two bands; dactyl greenish yellow. Eyestalk with a rose stripe on outer face and brown on inner; cornea black with gold flecks. Antennal flagellum translucent. Colour patterns difficult to see due to adherence of mud particles to the plumose setae.

Habitat—Muddy areas.

Size—Shield length: male 19.8 mm.

Range—Northwestern Pacific, Chukchi Sea, Bering Sea to off Santa Cruz, California; from 4 to 439 m.

Distribution in British Columbia—Common on muddy bottoms.

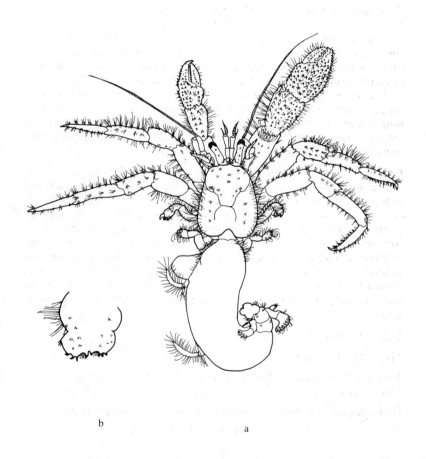

b

a

Fig. 58 *Pagurus caurinus*: a, male, dorsal view; b, telson.

153

Pagurus capillatus (Benedict 1892)
Eupagurus capillatus, Pagurus setosus

Description—Carapace: shield nearly as broad as long. Eyestalk slender and long; cornea slightly dilated. Surface spines on chelipeds are hidden by a dense covering of long, soft plumose setae; merus with a few small spines and tufts of long setae, distal margin with numerous small teeth; carpus setose with inner margin serrated with larger spines than those scattered over dorsal surface and outer margin; palm and fingers with setae covering many rows of spines. Hand of adult male proportionately longer than that of female. Left cheliped relatively small and slender with long fingers. 1st and 2nd walking legs slender and setose, with carpi, of 1st legs only, serrate on dorsal margins; dactyl long and slender, with minute movable spines on ventral margin; claw stout.

Colour—Carapace: shield cream with mottled red, brown, green, and cream mid-dorsally and laterally; posterior pink and brown. Abdomen pale pink with brown spots. Chelipeds: merus white with irregular bands of rose and brown; carpus white with apricot spines, brown and red mottled; hand light brown and fingers with apricot tips. Walking legs: ischium pink, red and yellow splotched; merus irregularly banded in red and brown; carpus and propodus each with two bands; dactyl greenish yellow. Eyestalk with a rose stripe on outer face and brown on inner; cornea black with gold flecks. Antennal flagellum translucent. Colour patterns difficult to see due to adherence of mud particles to the plumose setae.

Habitat—Muddy areas.

Size—Shield length: male 19.8 mm.

Range—Northwestern Pacific, Chukchi Sea, Bering Sea to off Santa Cruz, California; from 4 to 439 m.

Distribution in British Columbia—Common on muddy bottoms.

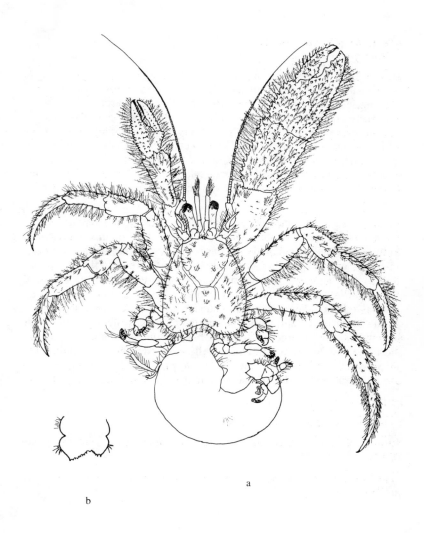

b

a

Fig. 59 *Pagurus capillatus*: a, male, dorsal view; b, telson.

Pagurus setosus (Benedict 1892)

Eupagurus setosus

Description—Carapace: shield subequal in length and width. Eyestalk stout, with cornea little dilated. Right cheliped setose, shorter than walking legs; merus with a few tufts of long setae; carpus with tufts of long setae encircling the large, curved corneous spines on inner margin; hand dorsally slightly convex with many spines ranging in size from minute to large, setose; fingers wide. Left cheliped similar but slender and almost as long as right. 1st and 2nd walking legs with tufts of long setae on margins, with only the dorsal margin of the carpus of right 1st leg serrate; dactyl longer than propodus, with stout movable spines ventrally; claw strong.

Colour—Carapace mottled red, white and brown, Abdomen red and white marbled and with white dots. Chelipeds: ischium pink; merus pink with red and white dots medially; carpus pink with proximal and medial red bands and opaque white dots; palm pink with a few red flecks; fingers orange with white calcareous and brown corneous teeth. Mud-coloured setae obscure much of the colour. Walking legs: ischium pink; merus mottled light and dark red, distally banded and with scattered white dots; carpus bands of red and white, or mottled red and white; propodus with narrow bands of mottled red, of wide bands of white, and of red mottled and of narrow white bands; dactyl yellow to red with small white dots medially; claw brown. Eyestalk red, white and tan with translucent dots; cornea black with gold flecks. Antennal flagellum translucent yellow.

Habitat—Rocks, mud or sand.

Size—Shield length: male 13.1 mm.

Range—Kodiak, Alaska, to off Santa Cruz Island, California; from 9 to 487 m.

Distribution in British Columbia—Widespread but not in great numbers.

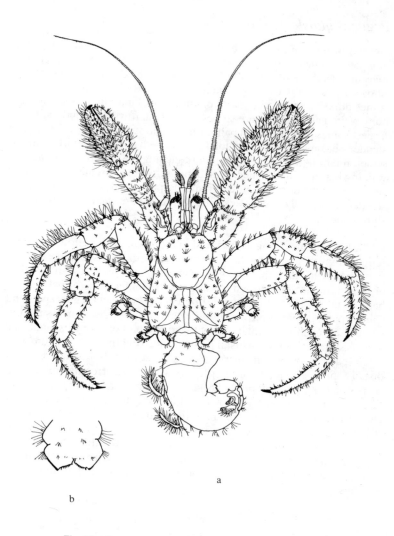

b

a

Fig. 60 *Pagurus setosus*: a, male, dorsal view; b, telson.

Pagurus quaylei Hart 1971

Description—Carapace: shield subequal in length and width. Eyestalk elongate; cornea slightly dilated; eyescale with 1 to 5 sharp-pointed marginal teeth. Right cheliped stout and shorter than walking legs, setose; merus with 1 or more large knobs ventrally; carpus with small spines dorsally and larger spines on inner distal margin; hand somewhat convex with numerous sharp spines in irregular rows, longitudinally, and largest spines on mid-dorsal palm; fingers short. Left cheliped, long and slender, setose and spinulose; long fingers with combs of short corneous setae on cutting surface, gaping and touching only at tips. 1st and 2nd walking legs long and slender with dense tufts of long setae, 1st legs with serrate margins dorsally on carpi and propodi; dactyls elongate; claws slender, curved. Dactyl of left 2nd leg may be armed with numerous spines and tubercles.

Colour—Carapace: shield dark red and brown, with yellow and pink reticulations medially; laterally dark brown with light spots; posteriorly pinkish brown with light blue spots. Right cheliped: ischium with patches of brown; merus dark brown with light spots and a white or pale brown band distally; carpus mottled grey or greenish-brown with grey spots and spines; palm greenish-brown with grey and white spines; fingers mainly white. Left cheliped similar except that distal part of carpus is white and there is some grey-blue on distal part of hand. Walking legs: ischium with a few patches of brown; merus with a band of red-brown, grey and, distally, pinkish white; carpus grey to white with irregular red-brown stripes on outer surface; propodus grey with 4 red-brown stripes on outer face, 1 on inner face and a yellowish white band distally; dactyl with dark grey patch proximally, a short red-brown stripe dorsally and a thin red stripe on each lateral face; claw brown. Eyestalk pale brown with red, brown and white dots; cornea black overlaid with silver except for 2 circular bands. Antennal flagellum translucent but irregularly banded with dark brown. Opaque white dots can be seen on living translucent sections.

Habitat—Gravel or sand in shallow water.

Size—Shield length: male 4.3 mm.

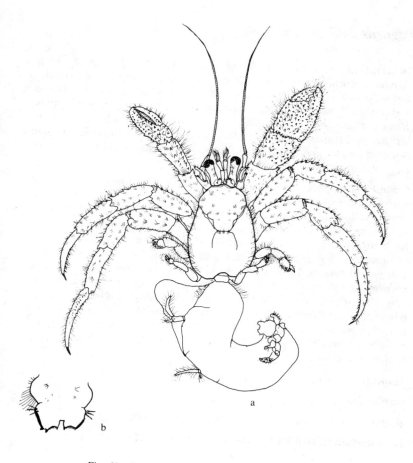

Fig. 61 *Pagurus quaylei*: a, male, dorsal view; b, telson.

Range—Point Cuerbo, San Fernando Island, Alaska (55°29′N, 130°19′W), to San Quentin Bay, Baja California, Mexico; intertidal to 97 m.

Distribution in British Columbia—Outer coast.

Pagurus dalli (Benedict 1892)
Eupagurus dalli

Description—Carapace: shield subequal in length and width. Eyestalk slender; cornea slightly dilated. Right cheliped with short setae, slender, and subequal in length to walking legs; merus short; carpus increases in width distally and both lateral margins are marked by a row of spines, dorsal surface with small spines and granules; hand slender, margin serrated and spines on dorsal surface. Left cheliped with spined median ridge on carpus, palm and fixed finger. 1st and 2nd walking legs stout; carpi serrate dorsally; dactyls long; claws sharp.

Colour—Carapace: shield network of white, tan, mahogany and red with an anterior margin scarlet; rest of carapace and abdomen cream, white, yellow, purple and red. Chelipeds: ischium white with fine red streaks; merus yellow-brown marbled with dark red granules and marginal teeth with a narrow white band distally; carpus and palm light brown or orange with grey or white, red tipped spines; fingers mostly orange with white spines. 1st and 2nd walking legs: ischium, flesh with fine network of red; merus, flesh with patches of red or yellow and opaque white distally; carpus mostly dark red with yellow patches; propodus purplish red and yellow; dactyl purplish-red proximally, then yellow and red; claw green. Eyestalk white with yellow brown bands proximally and distally, a row of red dots dorsally; cornea black. Antennal flagellum red brown and white dorsally.

Habitat—Gravel, sand or mud bottoms.

Size—Shield length: male 11.9 mm.

Range—Bering Sea to Oregon; intertidal to 276 m.

Distribution in British Columbia—Widespread but not abundant.

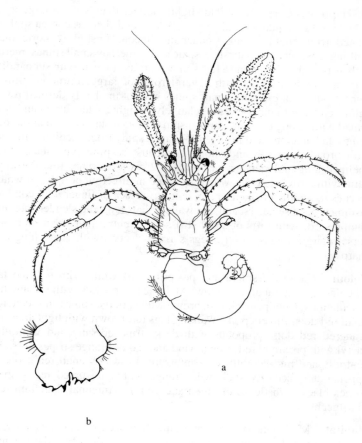

a

b

Fig. 62 *Pagurus dalli*: a, male, dorsal view; b, telson.

Pagurus stevensae Hart 1971
Pagurus brandti

Description—Carapace: shield slightly longer than wide in large individuals and subequal in small. Eyestalk long and slender; cornea slightly dilated. Right cheliped long, slender and subequal or slightly shorter than walking legs, surfaces with short setae and numerous small spines; merus with tufts of short setae and a few spines; carpus elongate with subparallel margins, inner margin with several rows of large, corneous-tipped spines, outer margin with small spines but not in clearly defined rows; palm slender with inner margin relatively straight, outer curved and both armed with strong corneous-tipped spines, dorsal surface with numerous spines and an elongated inverted V-shaped spiny ridge medially; fingers with broad flat teeth and short, corneous, rasping type setae. Left cheliped long and slender; carpus with 2 rows of spines mid-dorsally; palm with a row of spines which alternate in direction of tips and which reaches to middle of fixed finger, cutting surface of finger with comb of rasping type of setae. 1st and 2nd walking legs long and slender, laterally compressed, with tufts of short stiff setae, ventral margin of meri and dorsal margin of carpi of 1st legs serrate; dactyls with claws long and sharp.

Colour—Carapace: shield and posterior part white with red and tan reticulations; lateral areas yellow. Abdomen also white with red and tan reticulations. Chelipeds pinkish brown with dark red spines and scattered small red dots; fingers pink. Walking legs red-brown with light area and scattered red dots; propodus with dark stripe dorsally and ventrally; dactyl with proximal red-brown band and red or orange stripes dorsally, ventrally and mid-laterally with interrupted rows of small red spots on upper, outer face. Eyestalk pale orange with interrupted red stripes; cornea black with flecks of green and yellow. Antennal flagellum red, translucent.

Habitat—Mud, sand or gravel bottom; often occupy shell covered with living sponge, *Suberites ficus*, which ultimately dissolves the calcium carbonate of the shell. But the cavity is retained and increases in size with the growth of the crab.

Size—Shield length: male 11 mm.

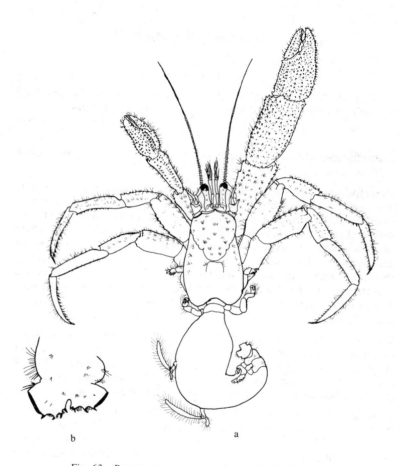

Fig. 63 *Pagurus stevensae*: a, male, dorsal view; b, telson.

Range—Akun Bay, Akun Island, Bering Sea, to Puget Sound, Washington; 13 to 198 m.

Distribution in British Columbia—Widespread but uncommon except for juveniles which are sometimes found in swarms in June and July.

Superfamily Hippidea

Family HIPPIDAE

Key to Species

1. Pereiopods flattened and modified for digging. Antennal flagella long and featherlike and hidden in mouth parts when not in use .... *Emerita analoga*

Emerita analoga (Stimpson 1857)   *Sand or Mole Crab*
Hippa analoga

Description—Egg-shaped. Carapace marked on anterior half with fine transverse striations; front tridentate. Eyestalk long and slender with a small, terminal cornea. Antennules slender and setose. Antennal flagella long and robust with double rows of plumose setae which are hidden beneath mouth parts except when animal actively feeding. First 4 pairs of pereiopods greatly modified and used for digging. They are heavily bristled, flattened and curved and not chelate. 5th pereiopod slender and chelate and used for cleaning as in other Anomura. Abdominal segments decrease in size posteriorly; telson large and arrow-head shaped. Uropods well developed but pleopods only in females; three pairs.

Colour—Carapace greenish or steel grey dorsally with fine cross stripes of lighter colour, or pink, anteriorly; posteriorly two white dots on light coloured mid-dorsal with pale pink laterally. First pereiopod shell pink and white; the rest mostly pink with some pale iridescence. Abdomen grey with 6th segment and telson white, with two pink stripes.

Habitat—Sandy beaches with heavy surf. These crabs bury themselves backwards in sand quickly to avoid being swept away by surf or current. On wet sand they move backwards leaving a typical track. They feed, when almost completely submerged, by unfurling the net made by the antennal flagella which filters plankton from the sea water.

Size—Carapace: male 22 mm; female 35 mm.

Range—Records from Karluk, Kodiak Island, Alaska, Wickaninnish Bay, Vancouver Island, and Kalalock Beach, Washington. All these appear to be individuals of a temporary invasion by planktonic larvae drifting north. They are not found regularly in these localities. Permanent

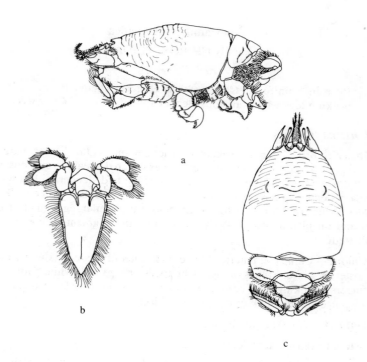

Fig. 64   *Emerita analoga*: a, female, lateral view; b, tail fan; c, female, dorsal view.

colonies are found from Oregon to Mexico, and from Peru, Chile and Argentina; intertidal.

Distribution in British Columbia—In the sand of Wickaninnish Bay, Vancouver Island, between 1958 and 1960, there were many individuals, but in 1961 I found only one large cast shell and I know of no record since. Old-time residents in the area tell of earlier invasions.

Notes—This species occurs in tremendous numbers in southern waters and is harvested for fish bait. Despite considerable research done by a number of people, the life history of this interesting species is still not at all clear.

Superfamily Galatheidea
Family CHIROSTYLIDAE
Key to Species

1. Rostrum spiniform. Carapace and elongate chelipeds and walking legs with numerous slender spines .... *Chirostylus* sp.

Chirostylus sp.

Description—Carapace subequal in length and width, lateral margins curved, surface covered with sharp spines which decrease in size posteriorly. Rostrum styliform. Chelipeds very long and slender with rows of sharp slender spines on all parts except fingers. Slender spined walking legs about ¾ length of chelipeds. Spines on abdominal segments 1, 2 and 6 and on pleural margins. Eyestalk short and pigmented; cornea not dilated.

Colour—Carapace: anterior bluish pink, laterally pale pink and white; posterior white. Spines orange. Chelipeds orange with white palms and fingers. Walking legs orange becoming paler on dactyls. Antennules, antennae and eyestalk orange: cornea black.

Habitat—Abyssal muddy sand.

Size—Carapace: female 19 × 17 mm.

Range—Southwestern Vancouver Island (48°13′N, 126°18.5′W), to west of the Columbia River mouth, Washington; from 914 to 951 m.

Distribution in British Columbia—As above, from 951 m.

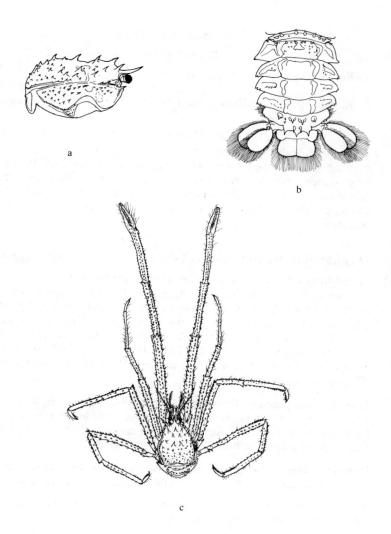

a

b

c

Fig. 65 *Chirostylus* sp.: a, female, carapace, lateral view; b, female, abdomen, dorsal view; c, female, dorsal view.

Family GALATHEIDAE

Key to Species

1. Rostrum spine-like. Eyes pigmented..
.... *Munida quadrispina composite*
1. Rostrum triangular. Eyes without pigment .... *Munidopsis quadrata*

The Genus *Munida* Leach 1820

Carapace sub-rectangular, convex, a few paired spines and lateral margins spined; surface rugose with fringes of short stiff setae. Rostrum long, slender and styliform, with a large spine (supraorbital) on either side of base. Chelipeds elongate and slender. Eyes large, well pigmented and dilated distally. May have rows of small spines on some abdominal segments.

Munida quadrispina Benedict 1902 — Squat Lobster

Description—Carapace longer than wide. 6 spines on gastric area; 4 in one line, and 1 on each side of the ridge near the hepatic region. 8 to 10 marginal spines. Rostrum long and compressed and minutely spined. Chelipeds with numerous spines and narrow fingers. Walking legs compressed and armed with short spines. Abdomen ridged but not spined except for minute spines on tail fan. Males with paired uniramous gonopods on 1st and 2nd abdominal segments. Female with small paired pleopods on segments 2 to 5.

Colour—Carapace and abdomen red-brown overall, ventrally lighter or white; ridges red with grooves white, and blue spots in cervical groove. Chelipeds with red spines; fingers red with distinct white tips. Walking legs with irregular light bands. Tail fan light coloured.

Habitat—Rocky areas, gravel, mud and sponge beds. They are predators on other crustacea and can do considerable damage in shrimp traps.

Size—Length 35 mm; large specimens, up to 67 mm, often taken in fjords, are probably an undescribed species.

Range—Sitka, Alaska, to Los Coronados Islands, Mexico; from 22 to 1463 m.

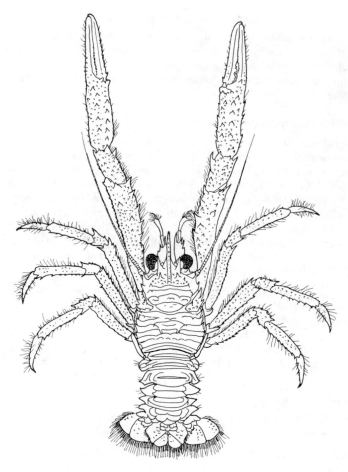

Fig. 66 *Munida quadrispina*: male, dorsal view.

Distribution in British Columbia—Type locality is Albatross Station 2878, off Cape Beale; 121 m. Widespread. A careful study of material at hand will probably reveal undescribed species.

The Genus *Munidopsis* Whiteaves 1874

Carapace more or less quadrilateral and relatively flat. Strongly calcified and usually rugose, spinose and tuberculate. Rostrum well developed, without large spines (superorbital) at base. Cornea of eyes opaque, without pigment. Abdominal segments often with spines or tubercles.

Munidopsis quadrata Faxon 1893

Description—Carapace nearly rectangular, with numerous granules. Rostrum triangular. Chelipeds long, with spines, granules and short setae; fingers flattened, shorter than palm and rounded terminally. Walking legs short, with scattered granules; propodus subequal to merus in length; dactyl with spined ventral margins and curved tip. Abdomen with granular patches, a median blunt tooth on 2nd, 3rd and 4th segments. Tail fan with telson composed of 9 plates. Male with paired gonopods on abdominal segments 1 and 2. Female with paired pleopods on segments 3 to 5. A few disproportionately large eggs are carried, indicating repression of the planktonic phase in development.

Colour—Carapace pinkish-tan with grooves white. Rostrum pink and white. Chelipeds white with faint tan areas and distal half of finger opaque white; ventrally, basis orange and ischium pink. Walking legs white and pale tan. Abdomen pinkish tan with white, medially; tips of spines and tubercles may be white. Tail fan translucent. Eyestalk pinkish tan; cornea bright orange internally and covered with a translucent white film.

Habitat—Mud and sand.

Size—Carapace: male 15.5 × 9 mm; female 13 × 8 mm. Total length: male 29 mm.

Range—Off Englefield Bay, Queen Charlotte Island (53°1.5′N, 132°54.3′W), British Columbia, to Tres Marias Islands, Mexico; from 86 to 1572 m.

Distribution in British Columbia—Off Englefield Bay, Queen Charlotte Islands, and SW of La Pérouse Bank.

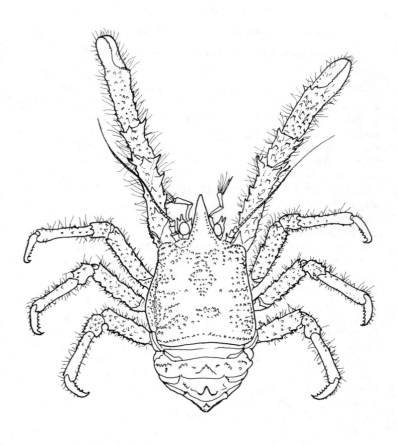

Fig. 67 *Munidopsis quadrata*: female, dorsal view.

171

SECTION BRACHYURA

Subsections Oxystomata and Brachygnatha
Superfamilies Oxyrhyncha and Brachyrhyncha

Key to Families

1. Margins of mouth parts taper narrowly towards front; triangular in outline .... Calappidae
1. Margins of mouth parts do not taper in front; square in outline 2
2. Carapace with front produced into sharp-pointed, paired horns or rostrum; may be partly or completely fused medially. Eyes not usually enclosed in orbits .... Majidae
2. Carapace with front not produced into a rostrum. Eyes usually enclosed in orbits 3
3. Front margin of carapace usually cut into teeth between eyes and on lateral margins 4
3. Front margin not cut into teeth between eyes and rarely on lateral margins 6
4. Carapace with uneven number of teeth between eyes; 6 or more teeth on lateral margin of carapace. Abdomen of male with 7 segments 5
4. Carapace with median notch on margin between eyes; 3 teeth or more on lateral margin. Abdomen of male with 5 segments .... Xanthidae
5. Carapace pentagonal with several spines on each marginal tooth. Surfaces covered with stiff club-shaped setae   Atelecyclidae
5. Carapace broadly oval with no more than 1 spine on each tooth. Setae, if present, soft .... Cancridae
6. Carapace subrectangular with distinct teeth on lateral margins .... Grapsidae
7. Carapace oval or round without teeth on lateral margins. Commensal or parasitic .... Pinnotheridae

Family CALAPPIDAE

Key to Species

1. Carapace oval with sharp-pointed projections on either side.
   Chelipeds compressed laterally and fingers meet vertically
   .... *Mursia gaudichaudi*

Mursia gaudichaudi (Milne Edwards 1837)
Platymera gaudichaudi

Description—Carapace finely granulate with symmetrical pattern of granulate knobs; lateral margins cut into numerous small teeth anterior to large sharp protruberance on either side. Chelipeds large and laterally compressed; hand with various sharp protruberances, granulate knobs and blunt teeth on dorsal margin and a granulated horizontal ridge on ventral outer face; fingers meet vertically. Right hand with a large basal cutting tooth on each finger. Blunt knobs on sternum adjacent to attachment of chelipeds. Walking legs compressed laterally, long and slender with narrow ridged dactyl. Eyestalk stout; cornea oval. First abdominal segment with a sharp horizontal ridge.

Colour—(Dead) Carapace white or pale yellow with numerous red granules which coalesce on outer margins, on small elevations and on the large lateral spines, to form darker red area; areas where granules are scarce or missing are white and some of these areas form a symmetrical pattern on centre of carapace. Chelipeds white, with red and pink patches and orange on inner surface of hand; outer ventral part, including crest and fixed finger are white; dactyl also white with some red spots on base. Walking legs red, pink and white with small red granules and areas of pearly opalescence; claw light brown. Abdomen pink and white.

Habitat—Subtidal areas of sand, mud or broken shell.

Size—Carapace: male 76.2 × 79 mm (width between tips of lateral spines); female 38 × 65 mm.

Range—Leonard Island ground, Tofino area, Vancouver Island, British Columbia (48°58′N, 126°10′W), to Talcahuano, Chile; 37 to 399 m.

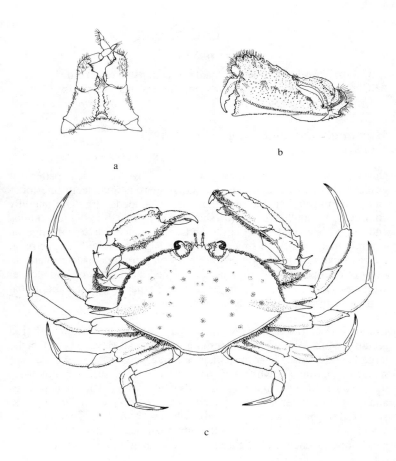

Fig. 68 *Mursia gaudichaudi*: a, buccal cavity; b, left cheliped, lateral view; c, male, dorsal view.

Distribution in British Columbia—One male, as above, is apparently the only record north of southern Oregon. It was taken in a shrimp net tow.

Family MAJIDAE

Key to Species

1. Body and appendages distinctly setose. Walking legs slender 2
1. Body and appendages with a few coarse and/or hooked setae 3
2. Rostral horns long, thin and parallel. Eyestalk long and thin .... *Oregonia gracilis*
2. Rostral horns short and divergent. Eyestalk short and stout .... *Oregonia bifurca*
3. Rostral horns long and divergent. Walking legs long, thin and rounded .... *Chorilia longipes*
3. Rostral horns short but may be wide and flattened. Walking legs relatively short and stout or, if long, laterally flattened 4
4. Surface of carapace smooth with hooked stiff setae to which material may be attached for camouflage 5
4. Surface of carapace granular and/or spiny 8
5. Carapace wider than long; outline shape of a maple leaf .... *Mimulus foliatus*
5. Carapace not wider than long; 2 large lobes or teeth on either side 6
6. Carapace with distinct constrictions between teeth on outer margins 7
6. Carapace subrectangular with faint constrictions between teeth on margins .... *Pugettia producta*
7. Longitudinal groove on ischium and exopodite of third maxilliped. Dorsal crest on merus of chelipeds *Pugettia gracilis*
7. Neither groove nor crest .... *Pugettia richii*
8. Carapace triangular or lyre-shaped. Walking legs short and rounded 9
8. Carapace sub-circular. Walking legs long and compressed laterally 10
9. Carapace triangular. Rostral horns wide with rounded lateral margins .... *Scyra acutifrons*
9. Carapace lyre-shaped. Rostral horns narrow with slightly curved lateral margins. Base of antenna with smooth round knob .... *Hyas lyratus*

10. Carapace with a few spines on anterior lateral margin. Meri of walking legs decrease in width distally. Branchial areas little dilated...*Chionoecetes bairdi*

10. Carapace with many large spines dorsally and on lateral margins. Meri of walking legs with margins parallel. Branchial areas dilated.. 11

11. Rows of large spines on dorsal carapace form a U. Deep groove mid-dorsally between branchial areas *Chionoecetes tanneri*

11. Rows of large spines on dorsal carapace form a V. Shallow groove mid-dorsally between branchial areas.........................
....*Chionoecetes angulatus*

The Genus *Oregonia* Dana 1851

Carapace subtriangular or suboblong, convex and tuberculate. Large spine behind eye (postorbital). Chelipeds elongate and walking legs slender.

Oregonia gracilis Dana 1851   Decorator Crab
Oregonia hirta, O. longimana

Description—Carapace subtriangular with numerous knobs with hooked setae or stiff bristles and slender elongate rostral horns. Chelipeds of mature male longer than walking legs, of female, shorter. Walking legs long and slender with numerous hooked setae and stiff bristles. Eyestalk slender, subequal in length to postorbital spines which are lanceolate and point forward; cornea spherical.

Colour—Carapace light brown or white with tan patches, masked by curved, brown hooked setae and bristles to which many dead or living objects are attached. Chelipeds white, mottled with light brown; finger pink or orange distally. Walking legs brown, deeper dorsally. Abdomen and sternum pale brown with some orange. Eyestalk grey and white; cornea red-brown.

Habitat—Intertidal in dense seaweed. Common in deeper water, in muddy, pebbled or rocky locations.

Size—Carapace: male 65.7 × 39 mm; female 45 × 33 mm.

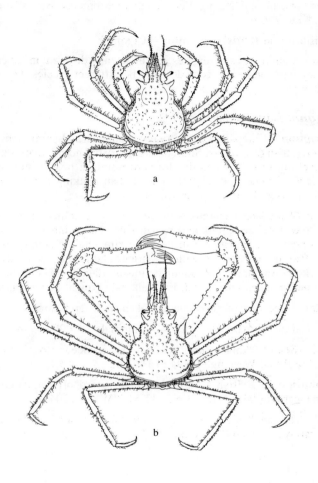

Fig. 69 *Oregonia gracilis*: a, female, dorsal view; b, male, dorsal view.

177

Range—Japan and Bering Sea, south to Monterey Bay, California; intertidal to 436 m.

Distribution in British Columbia—Common.

Notes—Adult males and females are sufficiently different in appearance that they were originally considered to be different species: *O. gracilis* and *O. hirta*.

Oregonia bifurca Rathbun 1902

Description—Carapace setose, finely granulate and spiny and wider, anteriorly, than *O. gracilis*. Short divergent rostral horns. Eyestalk short, not reaching tips of triangular forward pointing post-orbital spines. Chelipeds of male only slightly longer than walking legs; of female slightly shorter. All pereiopods setose.

Colour—Carapace deep pink with red patches; rostrum and post-orbital spines red. Chelipeds pink and brown with red on inner distal part of palm; fingers brown with red stripe on proximal half of both faces; teeth white. Walking legs brown with red stripes and patches ventrally; claw pale yellow. Antennule and antenna crimson; flagella translucent. Outer maxilliped crimson and brown. Eyestalk pale brown; cornea black.

Habitat—Deep water, green mud, broken shell, grey sand.

Size—Carapace: male 33.7 × 22.7 mm; female 29 × 20.6 mm.

Range—Sea of Okhotsk, northwestern Pacific Ocean, to off mouth of Columbia River, Washington 494 to 1463 m.

Distribution in British Columbia—One record off Englefield Bay, Queen Charlotte Islands (53°2'N, 132°51.8'W), at 1204 m.

Notes—The small size and deep-water habitat results in this species being rarely collected or recognized.

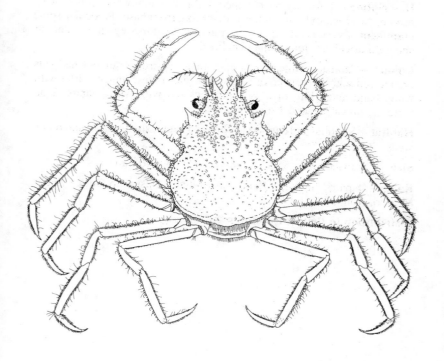

Fig. 70 *Oregonia bifurca*: female, dorsal view.

Chorilia longipes Dana 1851
Hyastenus longipes

Description—Carapace pear-shaped, inflated, knobby and spined. Rostrum of two long cylindrical horns diverging from base. Preocular spine prominent. Eyestalk short; cornea rounded. Walking legs long, smooth and cylindrical; 1st longer than cheliped.

Colour—Carapace white with orange spines; rostrum orange. Chelipeds orange-red with deepest colour on spines and ridges; finger scarlet with white band and white tips. Walking legs red with white bands: 2 on merus, 1 on carpus and 1 on propodus.

Habitat—Subtidal and deep water, on sand, mud, shell, gravel and rocky areas.

Size—Carapace: male 55 × 45 mm; female 54 × 40 mm.

Range—Japan; Shumagin Bank and Kodiak, Alaska, to Cortez Bank, Mexico; from 22 to 1 190 m.

Distribution in British Columbia—Common.

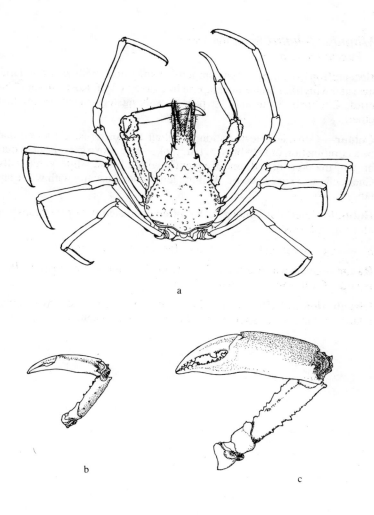

a

b

c

Fig. 71 *Chorilia longipes*: a, male, dorsal view; b, left cheliped, female, lateral view;
c, left cheliped, male, lateral view.

181

Mimulus foliatus Stimpson 1890*
Pugettia foliata

Description—Carapace flat, smooth, pentagonal, with margins laminate and winglike. Shape of carapace like a maple leaf. Rostrum short and bifid. Chelipeds stout and 1st pair of walking legs much longer than others.

Colour—Considerable variation in colour and patterns. Carapace may be a combination of kelp brown, tan, pink, white, dove grey, light to dark brown, maroon, or red, and frequently with a broad white V medially. Chelipeds also vary in color. Walking legs banded usually with white and tan.

Habitat—Intertidal, among rocks; often encrusted with bryozoans and other such forms.

Size—Carapace: male 35 × 39 mm; female 29 × 32.4 mm.

Range—Unalaska, Alaska, to Port Arguello, Santa Cruz and Santa Rosa Islands, California; intertidal to 128 m.

Distribution in British Columbia—Only on open coast of Vancouver Island as (far east as Sooke) and Queen Charlotte Islands.

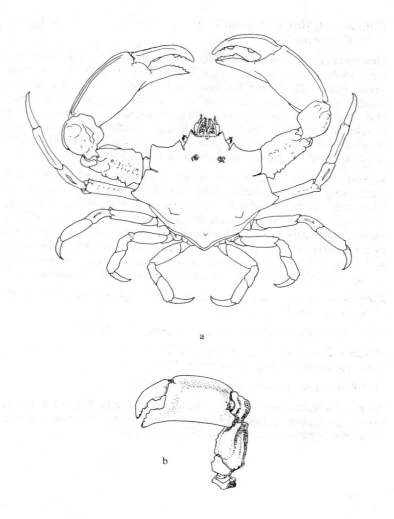

Fig. 72 *Mimulus foliatus*: a, male, dorsal view; b, left cheliped, male, lateral view.

Pugettia producta (Randall 1839)   Kelp Crab
Epialtus productus

Description—Carapace roughly quadrilateral, surface smooth with two large teeth on each lateral margin and with small preocular and post-ocular spines. Rostrum bifid with concave inner margins and hooked setae on dorsal surface of base and a few patches of small stubby setae. Hand smooth and palm slightly swollen; cutting teeth without any gape in female and immature male. In adult male, cheliped large and palm swollen with some gape between teeth. Walking legs subcylindrical, stout, and with strong curved claws with spines on ventral margins.

Colour—Carapace and dorsal surface of chelipeds and walking legs mainly kelp brown. Ventrally, chelipeds with some dark red on merus and palm with fingers red and scarlet with yellowish teeth. Walking legs with some dark red and yellow ventrally; dactyls greenish-brown and light brown; claws dark brown. Abdomen, with patches of deep yellow and light brown on sternum and outer maxillipeds; epistome brown with teeth and ridges red, scarlet or yellow, varying amount of dark red ventrally. Young kelp crabs are brown without the bright colours of adults.

Habitat—Among seaweed, especially bull kelp (*Nereocystis*). Adults often on piles under wharves.

Size—Carapace: male 107 × 93 mm; female 92 × 78 mm.

Range—Prince of Wales Island (55°26′N, 133°18′W), Alaska, to Asunción Point, Mexico; intertidal to 73 m.

Distribution in British Columbia—Common.

Notes—Carapace may be covered with barnacles in large specimens, but usually no organic matter is attached to hooked setae, in contrast to the camouflaging activities of *P. gracilis* and *P. richii*.

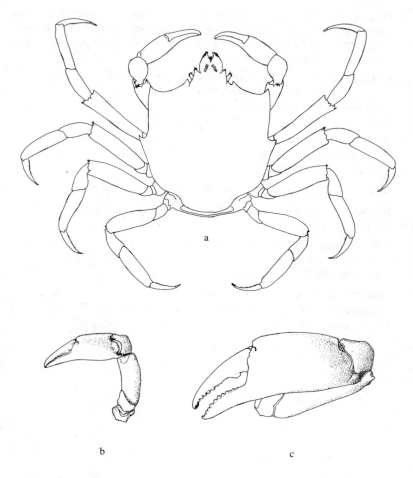

Fig. 73 *Pugettia producta*: a, female, dorsal view; b, left cheliped, female, lateral view; c, left cheliped, male, lateral view.

Pugettia gracilis Dana 1851*
Pugettia lordii

Description—Carapace with hepatic area greatly expanded. Ischium of outer maxillipeds and palp each with a longitudinal groove. Mature male with large cheliped; merus and carpus with 3 or 4 longitudinal sharp ridges; palm large and swollen.

Colour—Carapace, chelipeds and walking legs may be blue, brownish-green, kelp brown, red, pink, orange or opaque white in various combinations. Abdomen usually brown with 6th segment and telson white. Fingers dark grey or blue with orange tips and teeth.

Habitat—Common among eelgrass, kelp and encrusting algae in intertidal and subtidal. Carapace "decorated" with bits of algae and other objects.

Size—Carapace: male 53 × 34 mm; female 35 × 28 mm.

Range—Aleutian Islands, Alaska, to Monterey Bay, California; intertidal to 140 m.

Distribution in British Columbia—Common intertidally particularly in sheltered waters. On outer coasts *P. richii* seems to be the dominant form although *P. gracilis* is present.

Notes—The dark grey fingers and orange tips and teeth serve to distinguish living *P. gracilis* from *P. richii* which has violet or reddish fingers and white tips and teeth.

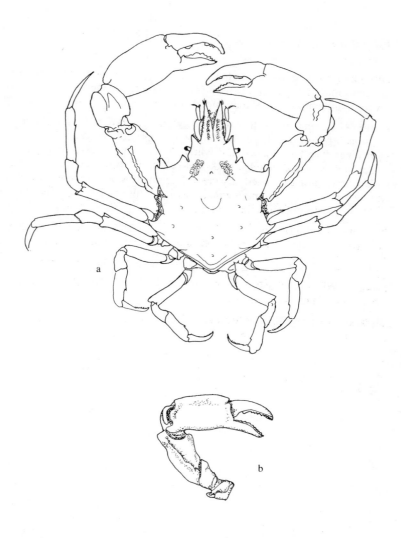

Fig. 74 *Pugettia gracilis*: a, male, dorsal view; b, right cheliped, female, lateral view.

Pugettia richii Dana 1851
Pugettia richi

Description—Carapace with hepatic area less expanded than *P. gracilis* and marginal projections narrower. No sharp ridges on merus of cheliped. Ischium and palp of outer maxilliped smooth.

Colour—Carapace purplish red with violet patches and white knobs. Chelipeds purplish red, yellow and white, particularly ventrally; palm with inner face pale brown and white; outer purple-brown and white; fingers pale violet with red streaks; teeth white. Walking legs red-brown, with a dirty white band medially on each segment; ventrally mostly white and violet. Antennules and antennae violet, white and brown. Eyestalk violet and white; cornea black with gold flecks.

Habitat—Common intertidally on open coast amongst algae and eelgrass. Often decorated with coralline algae, bryozoans, etc.

Size—Carapace: male 48.7 × 32.6 mm; female 33 × 26.5 mm.

Range—Prince of Wales Island (54°43′N, 132°17′W), Alaska, to San Geronimo Island, Mexico; intertidal to 97 m.

Distribution in British Columbia—Outer coasts.

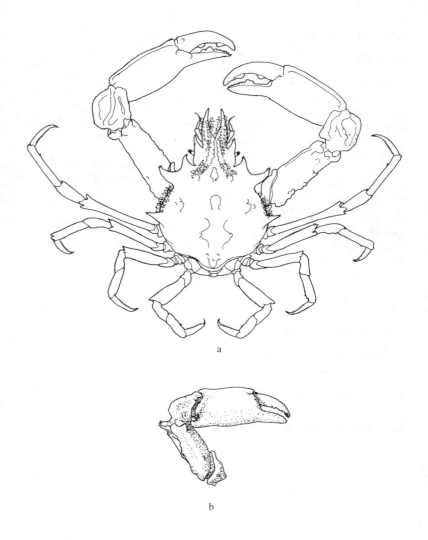

Fig. 75 *Pugettia richii*: a, male, dorsal view; b, right cheliped, female, lateral view.

Scyra acutifrons Dana 1851*   Sharp-nosed Crab

Description—Carapace somewhat triangular and thick with grooves, knobs and lumps symmetrically arranged. Rostrum of two horns, wide and flattened with divergent tips. Hooked setae on carapace, seldom used for decoration, but the surface is often encrusted by a growth of bryozoa, hydroids and sponges. Chelipeds large in mature male with numerous blunt knobs on ischium, merus and carpus, in rows on margins and scattered in between. Hand elongate, with sharp dorsal and ventral ridges; fingers slender with gape; dactyl with small teeth distally and 1 large tooth medially. Walking legs short and relatively stout, with short, stiff, club-shaped setae; dactyl about ½ the length of propodus. Abdomen of male narrow with 3 flat knobs per segment; telson smooth and triangular. Eyes small. Antenna short, flat and hidden under rostrum.

Colour—Often masked by encrusting growths. Carapace usually bluish white with blue-tipped, brown granules. A mature male may be deep red, brown or purple-brown. Chelipeds brown with blue or red granules; palm brown to orange; fingers orange red or pink; teeth white. Walking legs irregularly banded with dark and light brown; dactyl reddish; claw yellow. Antennular peduncle striped with light and dark brown; flagella orange. Antennal peduncle white and flagellum red. Eyestalk grey; cornea opalescent pink with black pigment spot.

Habitat—Rocky shores and loose rocks.

Size—Carapace: male 55 × 45 mm; female 41.2 × 30 mm.

Range—Japan; Kodiak, Alaska, to San Carlos Point, Mexico; intertidal to 220 m.

Distribution in British Columbia—Common.

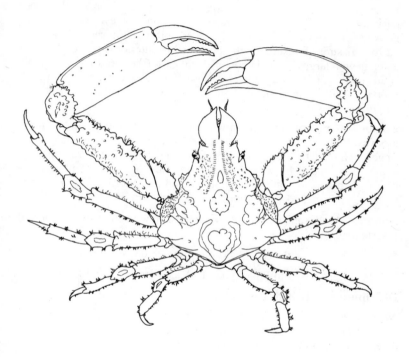

Fig. 76 *Scyra acutifrons*: male, dorsal view.

Hyas lyratus Dana 1851
Sayas lyratus

Description—Carapace sub-lyrate in shape; fine granules over surface which is somewhat inflated medially and on branchial areas; elevations have rows of larger knobs. Carapace and appendages with numerous hooked setae dorsally. Rostrum flattened, bifid and horns separated by narrow fissure. Eyestalk with tubercle on anterior surface. Base of antenna with large rounded knob on distal part. Chelipeds of mature male stout and longer than walking legs; those of females and immature males, shorter. Walking legs slender and cylindrical, decreasing slightly in length posteriorly.

Colour—Carapace mud-brown with orange median stripe and white in grooves. Rostrum white and orange. Chelipeds white, brown and orange; fingers white with orange streaks; teeth and tips white. Walking legs white, orange and brown; claws tan. Antennules and antennae grey-brown with base of antennular flagella and antennal flagellum scarlet. Eyestalks brown and white; cornea yellowish with black slit.

Habitat—Mud, sand and rocks. Often masked with encrusting algae and invertebrates.

Size—Carapace: male 105 × 80 mm; female 63 × 46 mm.

Range—Bering Sea to Puget Sound, Washington, 9 to 640 m.

Distribution in British Columbia—Widely distributed.

Notes—*Hyas coarctatus aleutaceus* Brand is found in the waters of Arctic Alaska but is easily distinguished from *H. lyratus* because of the distinctive knob on the base of the antenna of the latter.

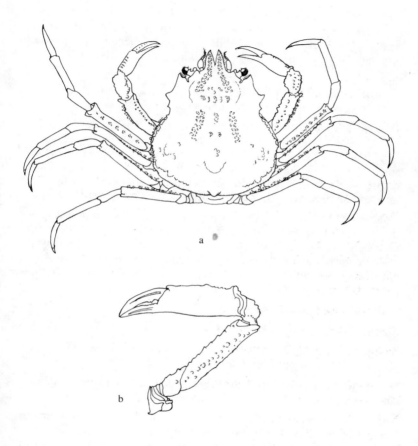

Fig. 77 *Hyas lyratus*: a, female, dorsal view; b, left cheliped, male, lateral view.

The Genus *Chionoecetes* Kröyer 1838

Carapace about as long as wide. Rostrum short with 2 flat triangular horns. Eyes large, in shallow orbits. Chelipeds much shorter than walking legs; fingers long and narrow. Walking legs compressed.

Chionoecetes bairdi Rathbun 1924

Chionoecetes opilio (British Columbia records), *C. tanneri*

Description—Carapace slightly wider than long with spines on anterior lateral margins; branchial areas slightly dilated but surface relatively flat with granular knobs forming a symmetrical pattern. Chelipeds short with small spines and granules; palm swollen and elongate; fingers with cutting surfaces of many small sharp teeth. Walking legs with merus inflated and margins with many small spines; carpus also spined.

Colour—Carapace greenish-brown with red granules and lateral spines orange, shell-pink and cream ventrally. Chelipeds with gold iridescence, pinkish brown dorsally with maroon spines; ventrally pink; fingers white with red stripes and orange at base. Walking legs brown, white, shell-pink and orange with red stripes dorsally; dactyls reddish. Eyestalk mud-brown and pink; cornea reddish with black pigment.

Habitat—Mud; usually in less than 200 m.

Size—Carapace: male 121 × 139.4 mm; female 74 × 81 mm.

Range—Southeastern Bering Sea, to Winchester Bay (43°34′N, 124°36.1′W), Oregon; from 6 to 474 m.

Distribution in British Columbia—In fjords and other muddy channels.

Notes—An arctic species, *C. opilio*, is found in shallow water in Bering Strait and around the Aleutian Islands. It differs from *C. bairdi* mainly in having length and width subequal in the carapace, which is also less spiny.

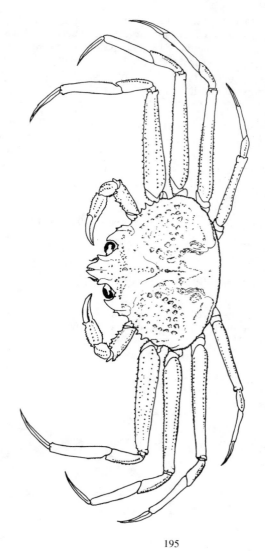

Fig. 78 *Chionoecetes bairdi*: female, dorsal view.

Chionoecetes tanneri 1893 Tanner Crab

Description—Carapace slightly wider than long; surface spinulose; margins armed with spines which are largest mid-laterally. Branchial areas dilated and separated medially by a deep depression; the rows of spines on each branchial area form a U with the curve at the outer margin and marked by 2 large spines. Hands of mature males with dilated palms. Walking legs compressed and have rows of sharp spines; meri slightly dilated.

Colour—Carapace scarlet, with some orange, pink and white in immatures. Chelipeds orange with scarlet spines; finger tips light pink with white cutting teeth. Walking legs scarlet with yellow-brown claws. Abdomen light orange or brownish. Antennules, antennae and eyestalks scarlet; cornea chocolate brown.

Habitat—Deep water, green mud, fine sand, rocks.

Size—Carapace: male 167 × 185 mm; female 119.2 × 114.8 mm.

Range—East of Kamtchatka, northwest Pacific Ocean, to off Cortez Bank, Mexico; 29 to 1944 m.

Distribution in British Columbia—West of the continental shelf from 458 to 1784 m.

Notes—Extensive studies have been made on *C. tanneri* off the mouth of the Columbia River by W. T. Pereyra and others. A dense population was found in deep water.

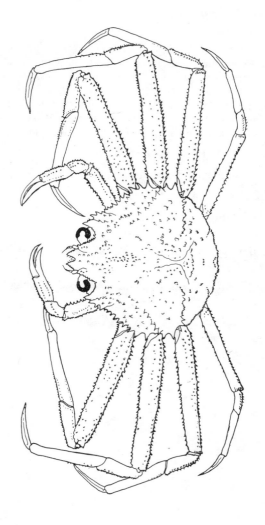

Fig. 79 *Chionoecetes tanneri*: male, dorsal view.

197

Chionoecetes angulatus Rathbun 1925
Chionoecetes tanneri

Description—Carapace slightly wider than long, surface finely pubescent with numerous spines and granules; lateral margins armed with large spines and posterior with granules. There are two rows of spines on each branchial area which meet to form a V at an angle of about 45°; the junction is marked with a stout spine on the lateral margin. Branchial area dilated but interbranchial space little depressed. Walking legs compressed with rows of sharp spines; meri slightly dilated proximally.

Colour—Adults scarlet; juveniles white.

Habitat—Deep water, soft bottom, mud, sand or ooze.

Size—Carapace: male 135 × 152 mm.

Range—Sea of Okhotsk and Bering Sea to Oregon, (43°01'N); from 90 to 2974 m.

Distribution in British Columbia—West of continental shelf from 1069 to 2430 m.

Notes—Easily confused with *C. tanneri* but usually caught in deeper water.

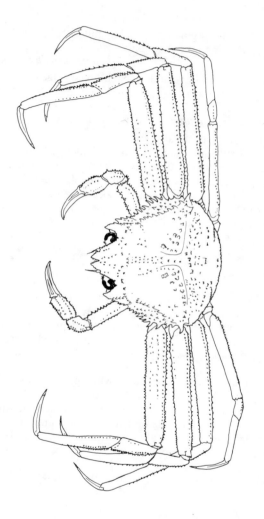

Fig. 80 *Chionoecetes angulatus*: male, dorsal view.

Family XANTHIDAE

Key to Species

1. Carpi of chelipeds with irregular knob and granules. Bilobed ridge on carpi of walking legs. Subtidal ....
.... *Lophopanopeus bellus diegensis*
1. Carpi of chelipeds smooth or wrinkled. No bilobed ridge on carpi of walking legs. Littoral .... *Lophopanopeus bellus bellus*

The Genus *Lophopanopeus* Rathbun 1898

Carapace hexagonal; front divided by small median notch; antero-lateral margin with 3 subequal teeth. Carpus of cheliped longer than wide. Walking legs stout with crests, especially on carpus. In male 3rd, 4th and 5th segments of abdomen coalesced making abdomen 5-jointed. Rathbun (1930) lists 10, apparently different, species of Lophopanopeus from the west coast of North America. Menzies (1948) did a revision and reduced this number to three, two of which have two subspecies.

Lophopanopeus bellus diegensis Rathbun 1900
Lophopanopeus diegensis

Description—Carapace surface with fine granules on margins and ridges. Cheliped stout with many knobs and granules on the outer surfaces. Dorsally carpus of each walking leg has 2 prominent naked crests; propodus may have 1. Carpus, propodus and dactyl of walking legs with short, dense pubescence.

Colour—Carapace mud-coloured with small white patches, and orange on median depressions. Chelipeds light brown, orange and white, with orange and maroon knobs; palm white, orange and maroon; fingers black. Ventrally white with a few pale orange spots. Peduncle of antennules banded with dark brown and yellow or orange. Eyestalk brown; cornea with black and yellow pigment.

Habitat—Littoral in California; subtidal in northern waters, in sand, mud or gravel.

Size—Carapace: male 21.8 × 25 mm.

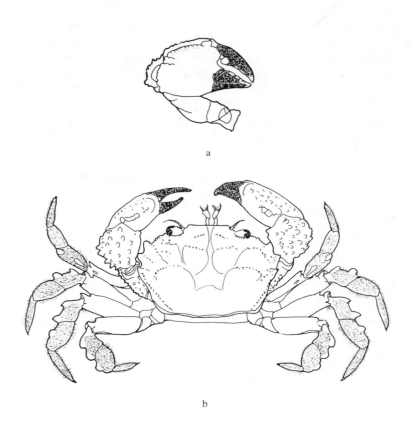

a

b

Fig. 81 *Lophopanopeus bellus diegensis*: a, right cheliped, male, lateral view;
b, male, dorsal view.

Range—Prince William Sound, Alaska, to San Diego, California; intertidal to 135 m.

Distribution in British Columbia—Widespread, but seldom collected;
from 9 to 135 m.

Lophopanopeus bellus bellus (Stimpson 1860) Black-clawed Crab
Xantho bella, Lophoxanthus bellus

Description—Carapace surface relatively smooth with a few small granules on flat elevations. Chelipeds stout with smooth surfaces; carpus may be slightly rugose. Walking legs stout with slight crest on dorsal margin of carpus. Some scattered setae and areas of short dense pubescence.

Colour—Variable. Carapace and chelipeds a mixture of various shades of brown, violet, purple, grey and white; fingers black with white teeth and sometimes with pink tips. Walking legs may appear to be somewhat banded with dark and light colouring. Ventrally light coloured. Peduncle of antennules banded light and dark. Eyestalk brown and white; cornea black.

Habitat—Intertidally under rocks in mud or gravel.

Size—Carapace: male 23 × 34.2 mm; female 15 × 22 mm.

Range—Resurrection Bay (59°56′N, 149°19′W), Alaska, to Point Sur, California; intertidal to 80 m.

Distribution in British Columbia—Common intertidally.

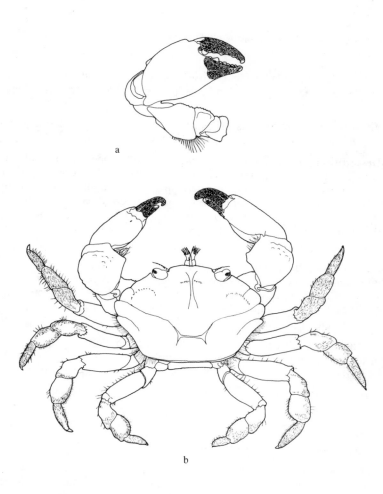

Fig. 82 *Lophopanopeus bellus bellus*: a, right cheliped, male, lateral view; b, male, dorsal view.

Family ATELECYCLIDAE

Key to Species

1. Antennal flagella long and setose. Cheliped spiny and short.
   Walking legs long, stout and subequal.............. *Telmessus cheiragonus*

Telmessus cheiragonus (Tilesius 1815)*   Horse or Helmet Crab
Cancer cheiragonus, Telmessus serratus

Description—Carapace broader than long and subpentagonal; all surfaces covered with minute spiny granules, stout club-shaped setae, and/or longer bristles on all margins and pereiopods; divided into 4 teeth; lateral margin with large triangular teeth, spined on anterior margin. Chelipeds short and spiny, with right larger than left and with more and larger teeth on cutting surfaces. Walking legs compressed laterally and 1st and 4th slightly shorter than others.

Colour—Carapace yellow with brownish or greenish areas; lateral margins scarlet and depressions light coloured. Chelipeds yellow with scarlet streaks and spots; fingers dark brown with a bright yellow spot; teeth grey. Walking legs yellow and brown with dark and light brown setae. Eyestalk greenish brown; cornea black.

Habitat—Usually subtidal, on sandy or muddy tideflats, among eelgrass or algae. During breeding season, in early spring, they may be found intertidally on rocks covered with algae.

Size—Carapace: male 83.5 × 97 mm; female 83 × 102 mm.

Range—Siberia; Japan; and Bering Sea to California; intertidal to 110 m.

Distribution in British Columbia—Common in suitable areas.

Notes—Well camouflaged and quick moving so that not seen often when alive. During the breeding season they moult and great numbers of the cast shells may form windrows on certain beaches. An allied species, *Erimacrus isenbeckii* is found in northern Pacific Ocean waters and used for canning and sold under the name of Snow Crab.

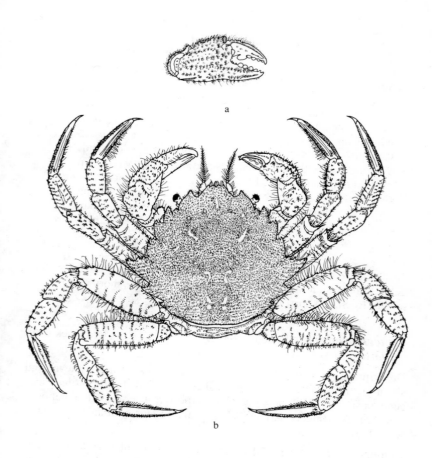

Fig. 83 *Telmessus cheiragonus*: a, right hand, male, lateral view; b, male, dorsal view.

Family CANCRIDAE

Key to Species

1. Fingers of chelipeds with tips dark coloured 2
1. Fingers of chelipeds not dark coloured 4
2. Surface of carapace relatively smooth; front of 5 subequal
   teeth .... *Cancer productus*
2. Surface of carapace not smooth; front of 5 unequal teeth 3
3. Surface of carapace setose and granules small. Cheliped with
   spines on dorsal margin of finger .... *Cancer branneri*
3. Surface of carapace not setose and granules large. Cheliped
   without spines on dorsal margin of finger .... *Cancer oregonensis*
4. Chelipeds with numerous teeth on upper margins of hand.
   Walking legs with setose margins and wide flat dactyls. Tip
   of telson of male rounded .... *Cancer magister*
4. Chelipeds with few teeth on upper margins of hand. Walking
   legs with naked margins and slender pointed dactyls. Tip of
   telson of male pointed .... *Cancer gracilis*

The Genus *Cancer* Linnaeus 1758

Carapace broadly oval; front with uneven number of teeth. Antennules fold back longitudinally. Antennal flagellum short and usually setose. Eyestalk short.

Cancer productus Randall 1839   Red Rock Crab
Platycarcinus productus, Cancer perlatus

Description—Front with 5 subequal teeth. Carapace surface uneven and slightly convex; antero-lateral teeth shallow, rounded and become more acute posteriorly with only one obscure postero-lateral tooth. Chelipeds stout, rugose; fingers dark coloured. Walking legs with dactyls fringed with short stiff setae.

Colour—Carapace dark red with white or red granules on yellow spots on elevations; front dark brown with white or pink granules. Chelipeds white, tan, orange, dark red and purple-red; fingers and teeth tan, tips blue grey or black. Ventrally, white with patches of orange and red with bluish granules. Eyestalk white with irregular red bands; cornea black

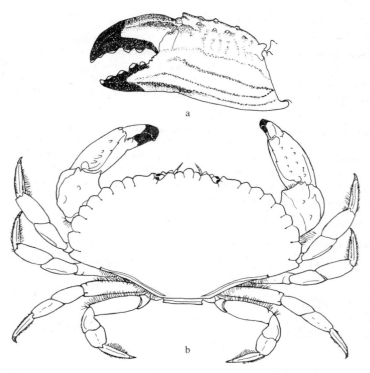

Fig. 84 *Cancer productus*: a, left hand, male, lateral view; b, male, dorsal view.

with gold flecks. Juveniles with carapace varicoloured, often symmetrically striped in dark and light colours.

Habitat—Rocky shores, hidden under rocks or partly buried under gravel or mud.

Size—Carapace: male 103 × 180 mm; female 81 × 158 mm.

Range—Kodiak, Alaska, to Laguna Beach, California; intertidal to 79 m.

Distribution in British Columbia—Widespread and common.

Cancer branneri Rathbun 1926
Cancer gibbosulus

Description—Carapace with granular surface, setose and uneven; antero-lateral margin cut into pointed teeth and postero-lateral with one tooth; margins meet at a distinct angle. Chelipeds setose covering rows of sharp spines; finger tips dark coloured. Walking legs setose; dactyl long and slender.

Colour—Considerable variation. Carapace yellow, tan, dark red, violet, grey, black and opaque white with varying combinations and symmetrical patterns. Chelipeds white and tan with red bands; palm yellowish and orange with violet spines; fingers white and brown with distal half black. Walking legs: meri white with two orange bands; the rest mostly red and lighter areas; claws yellow. Ventrally white.

Habitat—Mud, sand, gravel or shell bottoms.

Size—Carapace: male 49 × 58 mm; female 35 × 52 mm.

Range—Granite Cove, Port Althorp, Alaska, to Santa Catalina Islands, California; intertidal to 179 m.

Distribution in British Columbia—Common on outer coasts subtidally.

Note—Rathbun (1926) found *C. gibbosulus* from Japan to be distinct from those of North America, which are *C. branneri*.

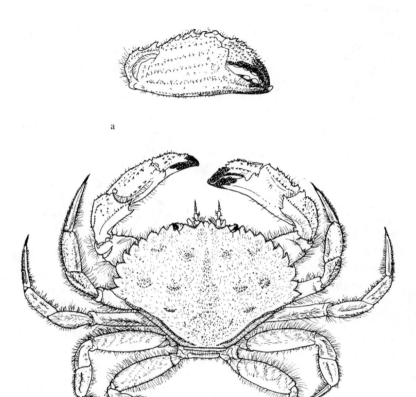

a

b

Fig. 85 *Cancer branneri*: a, right hand, male, lateral view; b, male, dorsal view.

Cancer oregonensis (Dana 1852)

Trichocera oregonensis, Trichocarcinus oregonensis, T. walkeri

Description—Carapace margins rounded, not clearly defined into anterior and posterior like other species of *Cancer*; margins toothed; surface finely granular, with knobs and grooves in symmetrical patterns. Chelipeds stout; fingers almost entirely dark coloured. Walking legs relatively slender and setose with stout dactyls. At least 3 variants may be found: The common form has marginal teeth on the carapace closely set and points curved. In the second form the teeth are flattened and joined laterally and the surface of the carapace has wart-like knobs. A third form has narrow teeth that are curved, pointed and separate and the surface of the carapace has numerous raised granulate surfaces.

Colour—Carapace mostly red-brown with grey granules and white patches. Chelipeds white with orange, flesh and pale grey granules; fingers black. Walking legs white with red spots and a web of purple, tan and flesh with grey; claws yellow. Abdomen white. Eyestalk white or flesh with light brown knobs; cornea grey with black centre.

Habitat—Intertidally in rocky areas under loose rocks or in hidden crevices under kelp holdfasts where their movements apparently make a "cave" from which they do not escape due to normal increase in size. Unoccupied holes in sandstone, originally made by sea urchins, and empty barnacle shells are also occupied. When these crabs cut burrows in styrofoam floats they can cause a serious reduction in the efficiency of floatation.

Size—Carapace: male 36 × 49.5 mm; female 31 × 42 mm.

Range—Bering Sea, to Santa Barbara, California; intertidal to 436 m.

Distribution in British Columbia—Common to 125 m.

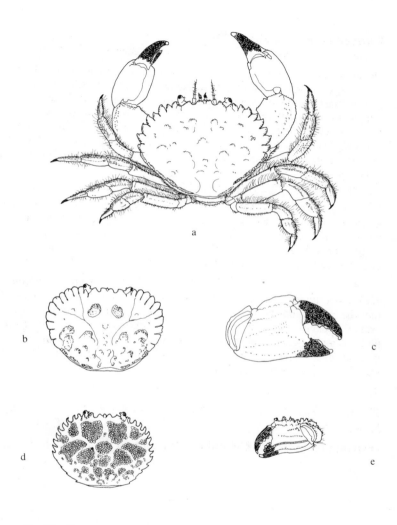

Fig. 86 *Cancer oregonensis*: a, male, variant 1, dorsal view; b, carapace, male,
variant 2; c, right hand, male, variant 1, lateral view; d, carapace, male, variant 3; e, left
hand, female, variant 3, lateral view.

211

Cancer magister Dana 1852

Commercial Crab,
Dungeness Crab, Pacific Crab

Description—Surface of carapace uneven, finely granular and slightly convex, with sharp teeth on antero-lateral margin, no teeth on postero-lateral margin. Pterygostomian area covered with a dense pubescence which apparently serves to prevent sand from covering the gills when the crab has buried itself for protection from predators. Chelipeds spiny and palm with dorsal margin toothed as is the finger; fingers light coloured. Walking legs broad and flat, last pair with propodus and dactyl particularly so.

Colour—Carapace brownish with pink or tan granules on ridges and ivory in grooved depressions, forming a symmetrical pattern; marginal granules ivory. Chelipeds with violet, dark brown, white and ivory granules on exposed areas and white on unexposed areas; fingers and cutting surfaces white. Walking legs ivory with pale brown, violet and tan streaks. Abdomen ivory. Eyestalk white with violet base; cornea black.

Habitat—Sand bottoms in which the crab may bury itself leaving only eyes, antennules and antennae visible. Water for respiration is drawn into the gill cavity and the pubescence prevents the sand from entering the branchial cavity. These crabs move very quickly, running on the tips of the walking legs and almost swimming as a result of the vibrations of the last pair of legs. They may also be found in muddy areas, but sand and eelgrass seem to be the preferred habitat.

Size—Carapace: male 160 × 230 mm; female 120 × 170 mm.

Range—Tanaga Island, Aleutian Islands, Alaska, to Magdalena Bay, Mexico; intertidal to 179 m.

Distribution in British Columbia—Widespread in suitable areas.

a

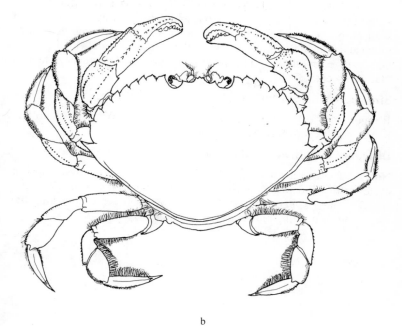

b

Fig. 87 *Cancer magister*: a, right hand, female, lateral view; b, female, dorsal view.

Cancer gracilis Dana 1852

Description—Carapace surface more convex than *Cancer magister* and finely granulated; front with 5 teeth, the central smallest; has sharp antero-lateral teeth and one small postero-lateral tooth on margins. Pterygostomian area pubescent. Chelipeds with marginal pointed projections, two blunt teeth on dorsal ridge and fingers subequal, with small teeth on dorsal finger and both fingers light coloured. Walking legs slender; dactyls cylindrical; claw sharp.

Colour—Carapace light purplish or red-brown with some cream-coloured granules; margins outlined with cream except posteriorly where they are beaded with purplish-brown. Cheliped: ischium white; merus with orange and brown spots; carpus and palm with outer face whitish with purple and inner faces violet; fingers white with purple-brown, violet and orange. Walking legs white with red-brown and violet streaks; claw orange. Eyestalk white with purple brown streak; cornea white with black crescent.

Size—Carapace: male 65 × 115; female 60 × 87 mm.

Range—Prince William Sound (60°46′N, 146°31′W), Alaska, to San Sebastian Viscaino Bay, Mexico; intertidal to 143 m.

Distribution in British Columbia—Common in muddy areas.

Notes—These crabs may eat up to 25% of newly settled oyster spat in oyster farms. Floating rafts for spat collection will thwart this activity. (D. B. Quayle, *pers. comm.*). They have been observed breaking the shells and then eating barnacles (Brent Cook *pers. comm.*).

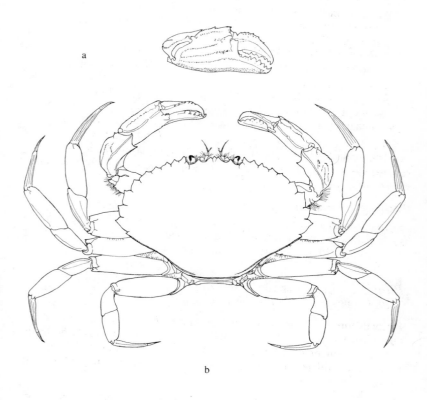

a

b

Fig. 88 *Cancer gracilis*: a, right hand, male, lateral view; b, male, dorsal view.

215

Family GRAPSIDAE

Key to Species

1. Meri of walking legs swollen and flattened. Can swim. Males without any pubescence on palms. Oceanic crabs 2
1. Meri of walking legs not so. Cannot swim. Males with pubescence on palms. Shore crabs 3
2. Carapace length subequal to width and lateral margins smoothly curved. Minute teeth on ventral margin of hand
   .... *Planes cyaneus*
2. Carapace length less than width and lateral margins straight. No teeth on ventral margin of hand .... *Planes marinus*
3. Notch on margin in front between eyes. Walking legs setose
   .... *Hemigrapsus oregonensis*
3. No notch on margin of front between eyes. Walking legs naked .... *Hemigrapsus nudus*

The Genus *Planes* Leach 1825

Oceanic or pelagic crabs. Carapace smooth, subquadrate or suborbicular, with a small notch or tooth on lateral margin. Chelipeds smooth with palm somewhat inflated. Walking legs broad and modified for swimming, with rows of stiff, swimming setae.

Planes cyaneus Dana 1852

Planes minutus, Nautilograpsus minutus

Description—Carapace subequal in length and width; lateral margins curved; front depressed slightly and faintly striated laterally. Chelipeds with fixed finger bent downwards. Walking legs flattened with naked merus much dilated; carpus, propodus and dactyl not dilated but with dense rows of swimming setae.

Colour—Variable; dark blue (cyaneus), blue grey, light to chocolate brown and white; dorsal surfaces may be of one colour, or the carapace, chelipeds and walking legs may be a mixture with mottled patterns and spots. Ventral surface pale brown, blue or white.

Habitat—Pelagic; on drifting debris, Japanese fishing floats, wood, green turtles, By-the-wind sailor, *Velella*, and kelp.

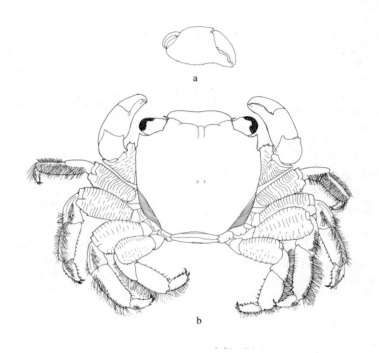

Fig. 89 *Planes cyaneus*: a, right hand, male, lateral view; b, male, dorsal view.

Size—Carapace: male 25 × 25 mm; female 26 × 26 mm.

Range—Eastern Pacific, Indian and South Atlantic oceans (St. Helena Island); Pelagic but occasionally found washed up on beach.

Distribution in British Columbia—On Japanese glass floats in the Juan de Fuca Strait.

Notes—Until Chace (1951) published a revision of the genus, there was considerable confusion in identification; therefore early records are suspect.

Planes marinus Rathbun 1914
Pachygrapsus marinus

Description—Carapace wider than long; lateral margins straight; lateral areas distinctly striate. Cheliped with fixed finger not bent downwards. Walking legs flattened; merus naked and dilated; carpus, propodus and dactyl not dilated but with dense rows of swimming setae.

Colour—Variable, especially in intensity. Carapace bright red-brown mottled, with dark striations, or chocolate-brown or light grey with pink tinge anteriorly. Cheliped grey with pink on merus and carpus. Walking legs somewhat banded with light and dark grey or shades of brown. Ventrally light brown.

Habitat—Pelagic; on floating objects such as fishing floats, buoys and Japanese mines.

Size—Carapace: male 17.6 × 19.9 mm; female 15 × 16.5 mm.

Range—Eastern Pacific Ocean, New Zealand and South Atlantic Ocean (St. Helena Island); pelagic, but may be occasionally washed ashore.

Distribution in British Columbia—Two records of specimens found on Japanese glass floats: one, 200 miles west of Vancouver Island; the other 20 miles west of Ucluelet, Vancouver Island.

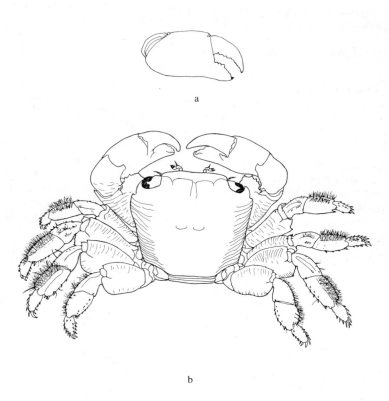

Fig. 90 *Planes marinus*: a, right hand, male, lateral view; b, male, dorsal view.

The Genus *Hemigrapsus* Dana 1851

Carapace subquadrate, slightly shorter than wide, antero-lateral margins toothed. Chelipeds stout with a patch of pubescence on inner side of hand of males. Walking legs stout and of moderate length.

Hemigrapsus oregonensis (Dana 1851)*   Green Shore Crab
Pseudograpsus oregonensis, Brachynotus oregonensis

Description—Carapace surface somewhat uneven; front with two lobes; antero-lateral margin almost straight and cut into 2 teeth which are more prominent than those of *H. nudus;* there is an impressed H medially. Chelipeds smooth, stout and with long fingers irregularly toothed. Walking legs with setose margins.

Colour—Great variation; patterns resemble pebbles, among which these animals are often found. Commonly carapace grey-green with dots and patches of light grey and brown with a narrow white, or light-coloured marginal band and white crescents posteriorly. White ventrally. Chelipeds white with green and brown areas; fingers light brown with

Fig. 91   *Hemigrapsus oregonensis*: male, dorsal view.

green streaks. Walking legs cream and green with dark brown or purplish pigment spots forming indistinct bands; dactyl light with 5 rows of dark seta. Eyestalk cream and grey with small dark brown dots; cornea black with silver flecks.

Habitat—Littoral and perhaps slightly lower intertidally than *H. nudus;* under rocks on muddy beaches, in short burrows on tide flats and muddy lagoon margins. They tolerate considerable brackish or fresh water and even short periods out of water.

Size—Carapace: male 36 × 49.5 mm; female 31 × 42 mm.

Range—Resurrection Bay (60°0'N, 149°17'W), Alaska, to Gulf of California, Mexico; intertidal.

Distribution in British Columbia—Common.

Hemigrapsus nudus (Dana 1851)* Purple Shore Crab
Pseudograpsus nudus, Heterograpsus nudus, Brachynotus nudus

Description—Carapace surface relatively flat and slightly convex anteriorly with a median H-shaped depression. Chelipeds smooth, stout; fingers long and irregularly toothed. Walking legs somewhat flattened, smooth, stout and naked.

Colour—Variable, especially in small individuals. Large males usually dark purplish red on the surface of the carapace and with pink or yellow granules in a symmetrical pattern of spots; narrow margins reddish with pale violet granules and yellowish streak posteriorly. Chelipeds reddish with purple splotches; palm violet with reddish spots; fingers violet to white and yellow ventrally, and pubescence pale brown. Walking legs dark purple with some red and yellow patches on joints; claw tan. Ventrally lighter. Eyestalk white, red and brown; cornea black. Occasionally one finds an olive green and yellow male.

Fig. 92 *Hemigrapsus nudus*: male, dorsal view.

Habitat—Upper intertidal, under rocks and gravel.

Size—Carapace: male 48 × 56.2 mm; female 28 × 34 mm.

Range—Yakobi Island (57°57′N, 135°23′W), Lisianski Strait, Alaska, to Turtle Bay, Mexico; intertidal.

Distribution in British Columbia—Common.

Family PINNOTHERIDAE

Key to Species

1. Carapace little, if any, wider than long. Last legs subequal in length to others 2
1. Carapace distinctly wider than long. Last legs shorter than others 6
2. Carapace hard 3
2. Carapace soft 4
3. Antero-lateral margins of carapace densely setose. Middle legs with fringe of plumose setae. Males and females free-living, or within the mantle cavity of a bivalve mollusc. Dactyls of walking legs strongly curved .... *Fabia subquadrata*
3. Not densely setose nor with swimming fringes. Live in ghost or mud shrimp burrows. Dactyls of walking legs slightly curved .... *Scleroplax granulata*
4. Longitudinal grooves running posteriorly from eye orbit. Second walking leg longest; dactyl distinctly curved. Females and immature males living within the mantle cavity of bivalve molluscs. Dactyls of walking legs strongly curved .... *Fabia subquadrata*
4. No longitudinal grooves. Last walking leg longest or subequal to first. Dactyls straight or nearly so 5
5. Dactyls of last legs subequal to others. Two small knobs on cardiac region. Live inside ascidians .... *Pinnotheres taylori*
5. Dactyls of last legs longer than those of other legs. No knobs on carapace. Live inside ascidians *Pinnotheres pugettensis*
6. Dactyls of walking legs with corneous tips strongly curved 7
6. Dactyls of walking legs with corneous tips straight or nearly so 8
7. Outer margin of eye orbit rounded. Male with tooth on finger of hand and a gape when closed; female without tooth or gape. Live inside clams .... *Pinnixa faba*
7. Outer margin of eye orbit angled. Male and female without tooth on finger of hand and no gape when closed. Live inside clams .... *Pinnixa littoralis*

8. Propodi of last 3 pairs of walking legs much wider and longer than dactyls. Fingers subequal in length and width and a central tooth on both. Live in terebellid worm tubes .... *Pinnixa tubicola*
8. Propodi of walking legs not so. Finger longer than fixed finger 9
9. Carapace with antero-lateral margin slightly granular laterally. No tooth on finger. No granules on carapace or appendages; margined with long plumose setae. Live in burrows of lug worm, *Abarenicola* .... *Pinnixa eburna*
9. Carapace with antero-lateral margin granulate. A central tooth on finger. Carapace and appendages granulate and margined with short stiff setae 10
10. Carapace surface uneven. Hand with palm increasing in width distally. Fixed finger of male may be deflexed. 2 sharp ridges on cardiac area; curved in male and straight in female. Live in burrows of echiurid worms or free in mud .... *Pinnixa occidentalis*
10. Carapace surface smooth. Hand with palm not increasing in width distally. Fixed finger of male not deflexed. No sharp ridges on cardiac area. Live under rocks in muddy area or are commensal in ghost shrimp burrows, or with a cucumber, *Leptosynapta*, in muddy sand .... *Pinnixa schmitti*

Fabia subquadrata (Dana 1851)*

Raphnotus subquadrata, Pinnotheres concharum, Cryptophyrs concharum

Description—Carapace smooth, soft or hard, depending on stage of development; immatures are soft, with membranous, unpigmented subquadrate carapace without longitudinal grooves posterior to eye orbits; ovigerous females are similar but do have the longitudinal grooves and a transverse groove between the eyes. Chelipeds and walking legs are subcylindrical and sparsely setose; dactyls have curved claws. Males and females metamorphose to a hard stage very unlike the soft stages. The integument is calcified and the carapace smooth and subpentagonal with anterior margins densely pubescent, covering sulci and front projections. Chelipeds with patches of dense pubescence and tips of fingers crossed. Walking legs flattened, margins pubescent, with long rows of plumose swimming setae.

Colour—Soft stages: carapace translucent creamy white with frontial area slightly more opaque. In adult females the orange yolks of eggs in the ovaries may be seen through the integument. Cheliped opaque creamy white with yellow tinged fingers. Walking legs creamy white with yellow setae. Eyestalk translucent white; cornea scarlet with gold flecks. Hard stage: carapace opaque white with anterior areas mainly tan, and scarlet reticulations on cardiac and branchial areas. Pubescence a light tan. Chelipeds white with yellow and pale orange; carpus and fingers a bright orange with pale grey pubescence. Walking legs yellow with orange; claw brown and setae grey. Antennule, antennae and eyestalk orange; cornea black.

Habitat—Commensal or parasitic in bivalve molluscs; only one crab per host. Hard stages also free swimming with plankton.

Size—Carapace: male 7 × 7.3 mm; female 17 × 22 mm.

Range—Akutan Pass, Alaska, to San Diego, California; intertidal to 220 m.

Distribution in British Columbia—Common in the mussel *Modiolus modiolus*, intertidally and dredged, but also found in *Mytilus californianus, M. edulis, Tresus capax, Mya arenaria, Astarte compacta, Cardita ventricosa, Crenella columbia* and *Kellia* spp.

226

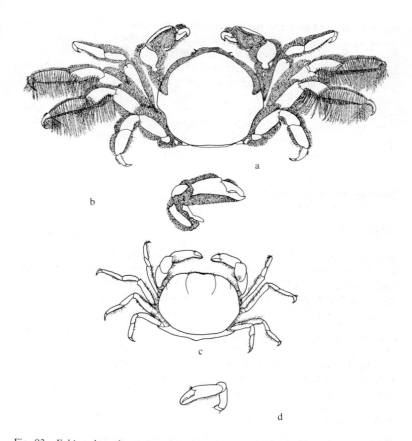

Fig. 93 *Fabia subquadrata*: a, male, dorsal view; b, right cheliped, male, lateral view; c, female, dorsal view; d, left cheliped, female, lateral view.

Notes—Pearce (1966) studied the biology of *Fabia subquadrata* from the waters of the San Juan Archipelago, Washington. The juvenile crabs settle to the bottom, after a free-swimming, plankton existence, and enter a molluscan host. There they develop a membranous integument and moult at least seven times. Then a dramatic change takes place when the next moult produces the hard stage described above. These crabs can swim well and apparently swarm and copulate in the early summer. The males are believed to die soon after but the females enter new hosts, moult and produce the soft stage again and lay eggs which are fertilized by the stored sperm. The hard stages were not recognized as the immature females and the males of *Fabia subquadrata* until 1928, more than 75 years after the mature female had been described. Because these crabs are given protection, take food and cause injury to the gills of their host with their sharp claws, they should be considered parasitic rather than harmless commensals, as some other pea crabs are.

Scleroplax granulata Rathbun 1893*
Scleroplax granulatus

Description—Carapace hard, convex, a little wider than long and smooth or finely granulate; lateral margins a smooth curve and there is a granulate ridge anteriorly. Chelipeds of female and immature male short and slender, with subequal fingers, small flattened cutting teeth and sharp tips. Cheliped of adult male stout, with swollen palm and fixed finger short and toothed; curved finger meshes with fixed finger. Walking legs subequal in length and tips of dactyls slightly curved.

Colour—Carapace white with a symmetrical pattern of dove or brownish grey; a narrow white, or light grey, band on all outer margins of carapace. Chelipeds white with grey or brown reticulations; fingers white. Walking legs white with grey and brown reticulations, becoming darker on distal part of merus and propodus; carpus and dactyl white so that appendage appears banded. Most segments have brownish dorsal and ventral margins. Eyestalk grey; cornea red with gold flecks.

Habit—Commensal in burrows of *Upogebia, Callianassa,* and *Urechis.*

Size—Carapace: male 7×11.5 mm; female 7.75×12.9 mm.

Range—Welcome Harbour (54°.05'N, 130°40'W), Porcher Island, British Columbia, to Ensenada, Mexico; intertidal to 55 m.

Distribution in British Columbia—Common on Vancouver Island beaches but few northern records, probably because these active crabs are inconspicuous on the sandy or muddy habitat.

228

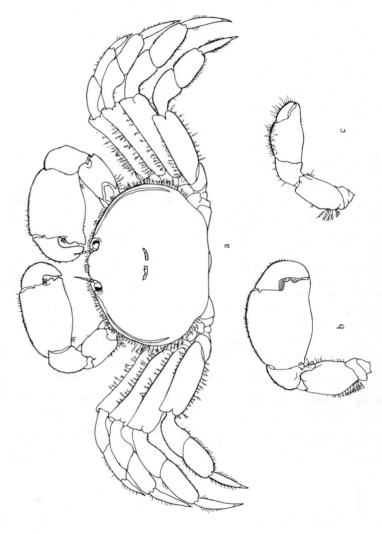

Fig. 94 *Scleroplax granulata*: a, male, dorsal view; b, right cheliped, male, lateral view; c, right cheliped, female, lateral view.

The Genus *Pinnotheres* Bosc 1801–1802

Adult females larger than males. Carapace poorly calcified, convex dorsally and elliptical. Front narrow and deflexed. Chelipeds short and stout. Walking legs subequal and relatively short. Abdomen may be broader than carapace and convex in female. Males and young females may have calcified carapace, be less convex, and front may be more produced. They can swim using fringes of plumose setae on walking legs. Abdomen narrow with 7 segments.

Pinnotheres taylori Rathbun 1918

Description—Carapace of both sexes subequal in length and width; there may be a pair of small tubercles on median cardiac area. First and last walking legs subequal and shorter than subequal 2nd and 3rd. Males covered by a short fine pubescence which is particularly dense on anterior margins of carapace and on all margins of appendages. Walking legs also have fringes of plumose swimming setae on the dorsal and ventral margins of carpus, propodus and dactyl.

Colour—Carapace of female yellow-brown integument and setae. Chelipeds of female yellow brown with brown reticulations. Male with red pubescence; fingers orange and tips white. Walking legs yellow with brown reticulations; dactyl bright yellow. Eyestalk yellowish; cornea red with a gold centre.

Habitat—Commensal in transparent ascidians *Corella willmeriana, Ascidia ceratodes* and *A. paratropa;* males much more active than females.

Size—Carapace: male 4.6 × 4.8 mm; female 7.2 × 7.5 mm.

Range—Quatsino Sound (50°30.4′N, 127°43.1′W), Vancouver Island, British Columbia, to Puget Sound, Washington; from 11 to 64 m.

Distribution in British Columbia—Recorded only from the southern part of British Columbia; possibly because it has been overlooked by collectors.

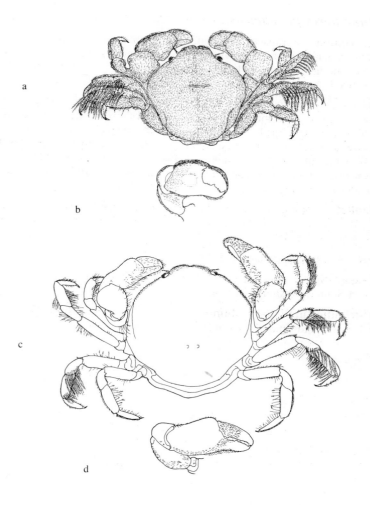

Fig. 95 *Pinnotheres taylori*: a, male, dorsal view; b, right cheliped, male, lateral view; c, female, dorsal view; d, right cheliped, female, lateral view.

Pinnotheres pugettensis Holmes 1900

Description—Carapace of female sub-pentagonal. Walking legs increase in length posteriorly with fringes of plumose setae on last 3 pairs. Dactyl of last leg much longer than others. The male has yet to be described.

Colour—Female carapace pinkish-purple with white overcast and yellowish sides, or light brown with fine dark brown dendritic chromatophores. Chelipeds straw-coloured and opaque white; palm pale yellow and light brown reticulations on outer face; fingers pale brown with white tips and teeth. Walking legs mostly straw-coloured but with some brown reticulations on white of last leg. Eyestalk yellowish; cornea red flecked with silver.

Habitat—Commensal in ascidians *Halocynthia hilgendorfi igaboja*, *Ascidia paratropa, Tethya aurantium* and the purple-hinged scallop, *Hinnites giganteus*.

Size—Carapace: female 12.5 × 13 mm.

Range—Spider Anchorage (51°45′N, 128°05′W), British Columbia, to Puget Sound, Washington; from 6 to 64 m.

Distribution in British Columbia—The only records are from the Strait of Georgia and Spider Anchorage.

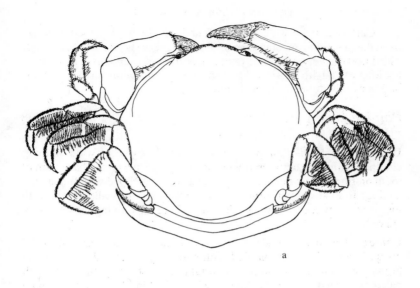

a

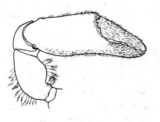

b

Fig. 96 *Pinnotheres pugettensis*: a, female, dorsal view; b, right cheliped, female, lateral view.

233

The Genus *Pinnixa* White 1846

Carapace much wider than long and may be hard or membranous; front narrow with a median groove. Eyestalk very short; cornea rounded. Third maxilliped with dactyl joined near base of propodus. 3rd walking leg longest and 4th shortest. Most species live as commensals within the body or in the tube of the host animal.

Pinnixa faba (Dana 1851)*   Pea Crab
Pinnothera faba, Pinnotheres faba

Description—*Male:* carapace firm and nearly twice as wide as long; cheliped with gape between fingers and only tips meet; may have a small tooth on finger. *Female:* carapace soft and oval; cheliped with fingers not gaping. Both sexes with rounded eye orbits and 3rd walking legs with merus about twice as long as wide; dactyls of all walking legs strongly curved.

Colour—Carapace of male bright tan with median and lateral patches of opaque ivory, light tan marbled with dark grey. Chelipeds white, light brown and orange with some fine bright tan spotting; palm white with pale orange and some grey, fingers white. Walking legs bright tan with lighter patches; claws translucent. Eyestalk tan; cornea black with gold or silver flecks. Female similar but overall colour less intense and ivory rather than white.

Habitat—In young stages found within many molluscs but a pair of adults is found only in one of the horse clams, *Tresus* (formerly *Schizotherus) capax* where the individuals mature. Immature individuals have been recorded in various clams: *Macoma nasuta, M. inquinata, M. secta, Mya arenaria, Saxidomus giganteus, Clinocardium nutalli, Serripes groenlandicus, Entodesma saxicola, Gari californica, Tapes japonica. Solen sicarius* and *Siliqua patula.* I have also found very young crabs in the sea cucumber *Cucumaria piperata* and the elimpet *Notoacmea scutum.*

Size—Carapace: male 10×17.5 mm; female 16×25 mm.

Range—Prince of Wales Island, Alaska, to Newport (Beach) Bay, California; intertidal.

Distribution in British Columbia—Widespread.

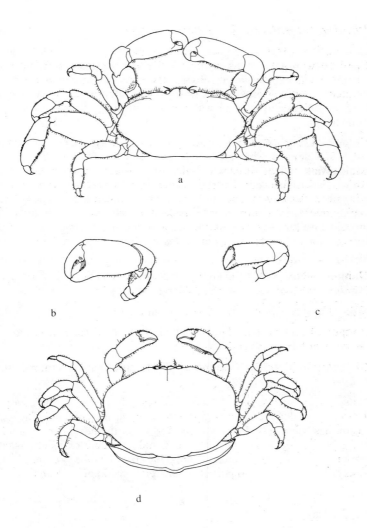

Fig. 97 *Pinnixa faba*: a, male, dorsal view; b, left cheliped, male, lateral view; c, left cheliped, female, lateral view; d, female, dorsal view.

Pinnixa littoralis Holmes 1894   Pea Crab

Description—*Male:* carapace firm and about twice as wide as long. Cheliped with gape between fingers. *Female:* carapace soft and oval. Cheliped with gaping fingers. Both sexes with outer margin of eye orbits pointed laterally. Merus of 3rd walking legs slightly less than twice as long as wide; dactyls of all walking legs strongly curved and sharply pointed.

Colour—Carapace of male opaque white with grey and brown marbled patches. Cheliped white with light grey and brown spots and fingers white. Walking legs white with light grey dots and streaks of tan; dactyl white; claw translucent. Eyestalk white with brown tinge; cornea black with silver flecks. Carapace of female with symmetrical patches of pale grey or marbled with brown. Cheliped white with some fine streaks of tan on palm. Walking legs white with pale grey and orange spots. 3rd walking legs with a yellow brown band on merus. Eyestalk white; cornea dark brown.

Habitat—Similar to *P. faba* but young may also be found in *Protothaca staminea, Panope generosa,* and *Ostrea lurida.*

Size—Carapace: male 10 × 18 mm; female 16 × 27 mm.

Range—Prince William Sound (60°33′N, 145°48′W), Alaska, to San Diego, California; intertidal to 91 m.

Distribution in British Columbia—Widespread but less common than *P. faba.*

Notes—*P. littoralis,* like *P. faba,* matures only in the mantle cavity of *Tresus capax* despite records in the literature to the contrary. This confusion has been caused by misidentification of the host. A pair of adult crabs, plus varying numbers of young and immature crabs are usually present in each clam, Pearce (1966: 579) considers the presence of the visceral fold or 'skirt' important in the relationship of crab host.

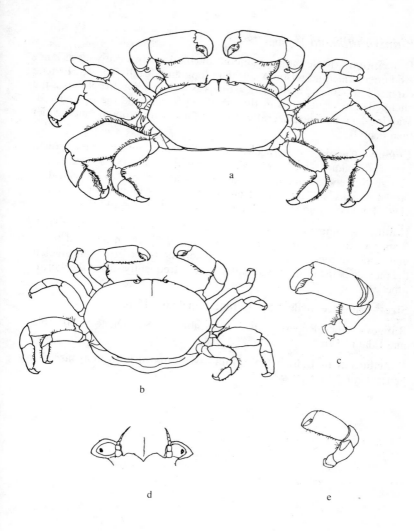

Fig. 98 *Pinnixa littoralis*: a, male, dorsal view; b, female, dorsal view; c, left cheliped, male, lateral view; d, anterior view, showing eye orbits; e, left cheliped, female, lateral view.

Pinnixa tubicola Holmes 1894*

Description—Male carapace smooth and hard and twice as wide as long. Abdomen wide and telson wider than long and distally curved. Female carapace smooth and hard and 2 ½ times as wide as long. In both sexes the chelipeds are stout, with median teeth on fingers and the tips curved. Walking legs flattened laterally and last three with propodi much wider than dactyls.

Colour—Carapace patterned symmetrically in light and dark brown, grey and opaque white. Chelipeds white with patches of brown, red or orange; fingers and teeth white distally. Walking legs white with dark brown streaks and reticulated areas; margins of joints white banded; claws light coloured. Eyestalk ivory; cornea red with gold flecks.

Habitat—Commensal in parchment-like tubes of terebellid worms. In British Columbia *Eupolymnia heterobranchia* is often attached to the undersides of rocks intertidally and broken shells and gravel are stuck to the outside of the tube. A pair of these crabs frequently shares the worm's tube.

Size—Carapace: male 4.5 × 10 mm; female 6 × 15 mm.

Range—Prince Rupert, British Columbia, to San Diego, California; intertidal to 57m.

Distribution in British Columbia—Widespread but often missed in general collecting.

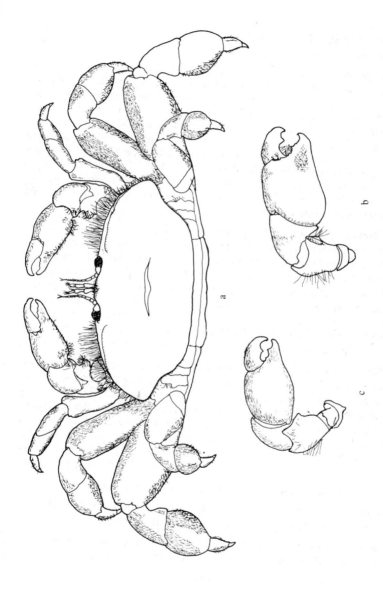

Fig. 99   *Pinnixa tubicola*: a, male, dorsal view; b, right cheliped, female, lateral view; c, right cheliped, male, lateral view.

Pinnixa eburna Wells 1928*
Pinnixa eburnea

Description—Both sexes with a hard smooth oval carapace with setose margins, an inconspicuous antero-lateral ridge which may be slightly granular on lateral margin, and a curved depression between gastric and cardiac areas. Walking legs and chelipeds margined with plumose setae. Walking legs slender, flattened; dactyls styliform. Mature males have swollen palms with a short, wide fixed finger; finger curved so that the tip crosses over the fixed finger and leaves a slight gape between. Females and immature males have slightly swollen palms with long fixed finger with curved tip; finger elongate and curved with a sharp tip which meshes with fixed finger and leaves no gape. The cutting surfaces are margined with a row of small stiff setae.

Colour—Carapace with a symmetrical dappled pattern of dark brown or black, red-brown and greenish-brown on white and ivory or yellow. There is a light border on all margins but the posterior. Chelipeds and walking legs pale yellow with patches of greenish-brown, making legs look banded. Patches are reticulated especially on carpus and propodus. Dorsally and ventrally legs are bordered with a narrow translucent area. Antennule, antenna and eyestalk yellow with black streaks; cornea black with gold flecks. Sternum and abdomen yellow or ivory with a few black specks. Considerable variation in depth of colour between individuals.

Habitat—Commensal in burrows of lug worms *Abarenicola claparedii vagabunda* and *A. c. oceanica*. Active when free in water but not when in exposed burrow. May be able to swim to some extent. Difficult to collect because the lug worm burrow is in loose sand or sandy mud and disintegrates easily. The crabs stay close to the worm; therefore, if the sand surrounding the worm is washed through a fine sieve the crabs may be captured. Small *P. schmitti* may occur in the top layers of muddy areas and can be confused with *P. eburna* until examined under magnification.

Size—Carapace: male 3.5 × 6.5 mm; female 3.5 × 8 mm.

Range—Masset, Queen Charlotte Islands, British Columbia, to False Bay, San Juan Island, Puget Sound, Washington; intertidal.

Distribution in British Columbia—Probably present where the host occurs but seldom collected unless searched for specifically.

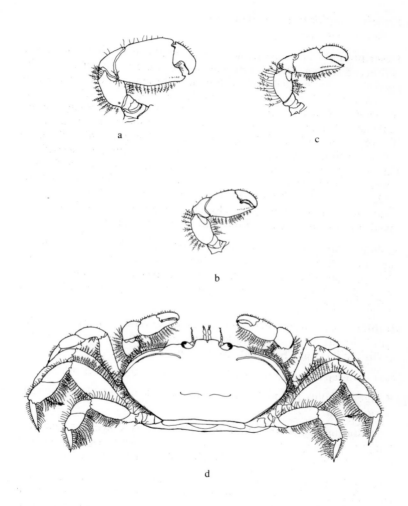

Fig. 100 *Pinnixa eburna*: a, right cheliped, male, lateral view; b, right cheliped, immature male, lateral view; c, right cheliped, female, lateral view; d, female, dorsal view.

Pinnixa occidentalis Rathbun 1893
Pinnixa californiensis

Description—Carapace narrows laterally and, in both sexes, the surface is firm and uneven. There is an acute transverse crest on cardiac area with curves on the male and relatively straight on the female. Anterior margins of carapace and the appendages are setose which is denser in small individuals than in large. Antero-lateral and pterygostomian margins granulate. Walking legs stout and elongate with numerous minute granules especially on dorsal and ventral margins. Merus of 3rd walking leg 2½ to 3½ times as long as wide; dactyls straight with granulate ridges. Cheliped of mature male with palm slightly widened distally with small granules dorsally and ventrally; fixed finger short and deflexed, with one large central tooth and small side teeth; finger curved and usually with as sharp central tooth; gape when closed. Cheliped of female with longer fixed finger than male and finger similar but less curved.

Colour—Mud and setae mask the colouring. Freshly moulted specimens have the carapace tan with some white areas in a symmetrical pattern. Chelipeds and walking legs white with small patches of tan on either side of junction between merus and carpus. Cornea of eye dark red. Ventral surfaces white.

Habitat—Commensal in tubes of unsegmented coelomate worms, (Phylum Echiura). In the northern localities this is *Echiurus echiurus alaskanus* but they may be found also free in mud.

Size—Carapace: male 9.5 × 19.5 mm, female 10.5 × 20.5 mm.

Range—Iliuliuk Harbor, Unalaska, to Magdalena Bay, Mexico; intertidal to 436 m.

Distribution in British Columbia—Dredged off Vancouver Island and found intertidally where the host occurs in northern British Columbia; collected at Welcome Harbour, Porcher Island and Digby Island.

Notes—Distribution records of *P. occidentalis* in the literature are suspect because there are other deep-water *Pinnixa* which resemble them but differ in that they mature at a smaller size and are less setose or granular. They are also usually a brighter colour, often scarlet. The body proportions are difficult to compare because of size differences. Until these

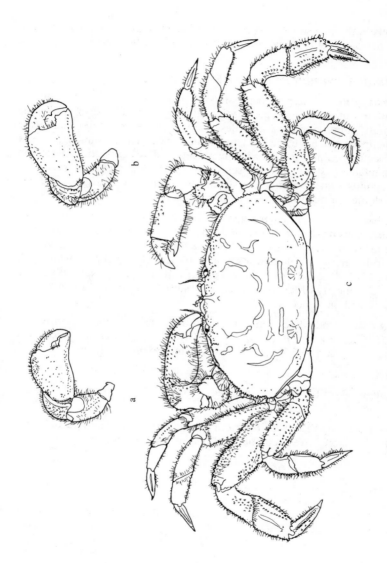

Fig. 101 *Pinnixa occidentalis*: a, right cheliped, female, lateral view; b, right cheliped, male, lateral view; c, female, dorsal view.

apparently undescribed species can be identified it seems wise to treat *P. occidentalis* as a key member of a group of allied species.

Pinnixa schmitti Rathbun 1918

Description—Carapace hard, smooth, about twice as wide as long and with a granular ridge on anterior lateral margins. Chelipeds of adult male robust; palm with a few granules; short fingers with small or no teeth. Chelipeds of female and immature male slender; palm granulate; fingers subequal cutting surfaces with small teeth and tips crossed. 3rd walking leg relatively stout and long, setose with granular margins on merus and propodus. Other walking legs slender and setose; dactyl slightly curved. Abdomen of male with a semicircular telson.

Colour—Colour often masked by muddy setae or stained by rust or sulphurous mud. In recently moulted specimens the carapace and dorsal surfaces of walking legs are blue-grey, black and white mottled; the margins are light coloured, especially posteriorly. Chelipeds white with fine black dendritic chromatophores dorsally; the palm, especially in the male, is mostly white, as are the ventral surfaces. Eyestalk brown; cornea black with gold flecks.

Habitat—Under rocks in mud or around worm tubes, in burrows of *Callianassa* and *Upogebia,* in sand with *Leptosynapta clarkii* (sea cucumber) and with *Amphiodia urtica* (burrowing brittle star).

Size—Carapace: male 5.5×10 mm; female 6.8×12.5 mm.

Range—Port Levasheff, Unalaska, to Morro Bay, California; intertidal to 146 m.

Distribution in British Columbia—Ubiquitous; small individuals common but large have been collected only in northern waters.

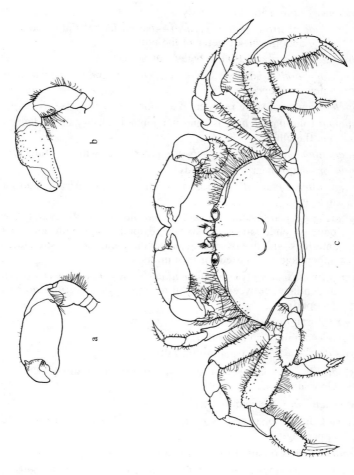

Fig. 102 *Pinnixa schmitti*: a, left cheliped, male, lateral view; b, left cheliped, female, lateral view; c, male, dorsal view.

GLOSSARY

Abdomen—posterior part of body.

Abdominal pleuron (plural: *pleura*)—paired lateral flat extensions on some abdominal segments of the body.

Abyssal—more than 2000 m below surface of sea.

Accessory tooth—adjacent to *crista dentata* on the inner margin of the outer maxilliped.

Acicle—antennal scale reduced to a spine.

Antenna (plural: *antennae*)—anterior jointed sensory appendage, with one flagellum.

Antennule—anterior jointed sensory appendage, with two flagella.

Anterior—at or near front of body.

Antero-lateral margin—region between front, or rostrum, and lateral margin.

Appendix interna (plural: *appendices internae*)—small separate appendage on endopod of 2nd to 5th pleopods. Tips with hooks which interlock with that of opposite appendage and serve to strengthen the appendage when used for swimming.

Appendix masculina (plural: *appendices masculinae*)—accessory male appendage between endopodite and *appendix interna* on 2nd pleopod.

Apex (plural: *apices* or *apexes*)—tip, top, peak.

Article—a unit of an appendage.

Articulation—a joint usually movable.

Ascidians—sea squirts of the Subphylum Urochordata, Phylum Chordata.

Asymmetrical—not symmetrical.

Basis (plural: *bases*) *basipodite*—second article from body of appendage.

Beaded—rows of small rounded knobs or granules.

Berried—describes a female crab with eggs attached to pleopods.

Bifid, bifurcate—divided by a deep cleft into two equal parts.

Bilateral symmetry—object can be divided into two equal parts.

Bilobed, bilobate—with two lobes.

Biramous—two-branched.

Branchial region or *area*—part of carapace covering branchiae or gills.

Bristle—stiff seta or hair.

Brood pouch—projection on female abdomen to protect incubating eggs.

Buccal cavity—cavity in which mouth parts are situated, surrounded by epistome.

Byssus threads—strong threads secreted by some bivalve molluscs (like mussels) which are used for attachment.

Calcareous or *calcified*—limy, containing carbonate of lime.

Capitate—having a distinct head: refers to specialized setae.

Carapace—exoskeleton covering head and thorax (cephalothorax).

Cardiac region or *area*—part of carapace covering heart.

Carcinology—study of Crustacea.

Carina or *carinate*—keel-like elevated ridge.

Carpus (plural: *carpi*)—5th article or segment of appendage.

Cervical groove—groove or series of grooves on carapace; may be transverse and oblique.

Chela (plural: *chelae*) and *chelate*—pincer, prehensile claw, "hand"; composed of propodus and dactyl.

Cheliped—whole appendage with chela or pincer.

Chitin—horny substance of exoskeletons of arthropods.

Chromatophore—a pigment cell in the integument which can disperse or concentrate the pigment to produce colour changes.

Clavate—club-shaped.

Claw—sharp corneous tip of dactyl of walking legs.

Columella groove—spiral groove around central axis of gastropod shell.

Comb—row of sharp spines.

Composite—made up of various parts.

Concave and *concavities*—outline, or surface, curved inwards.

Constricted—compressed or contracted.

Continental shelf—area from shore line to depth of 200 m.

Convex—outline, or surface curved outwards.

Copepod crustacea—small animals of Subclass Copepoda.

Cornea—transparent horny part of eyeball covering pigment.

Corneous—horn-like.

Corrugated—contracted into wrinkles or folds.

Coxa (plural: *coxae*)—first segment of appendage attached to body.

Crest—tuft or ridge.

Crista dentata—row of corneous teeth on inner margin of outer maxilliped.

Crustacean—animals of Class Crustacea, having hard outer shells and jointed appendages.

Cutting surface of teeth—inner margins of fingers of chela.

Dactyl or *dactylus* (plural: *dactyls* or *dactyli*)—claw, terminal or 7th article of pereiopod.

Decapoda or *decapod*—ten footed; an order of the Class Crustacea.

Deflected or *deflexed*—bent aside.

Dendritic—branching, tree-like figure.

Denticulated—with small teeth.

Detritus—finely divided organic matter from disintegrated animal and plant material.

Dilated—expanded or enlarged.

Dimorphism—two forms of the same species.

Distal—farthest from body; opposite of proximal.

Divergent—deflected.

Dorsal—upper surface of body, or back.

Elongate—longer than wide.

Endopod or *endopodite*—inner ramus of biramous appendage.

Epipodite—outgrowth of coxa of maxillipeds and some pereiopods.

Epistome—broad antero-ventral plate framing the buccal cavity.

Exopod or *expodite*—outer ramus of biramous appendage.

Eyescale—flattened projection at base of eyestalk.

Eyestalk—peduncle bearing cornea.

Exoskeleton—external skeleton of Crustacea; composed of chitin which may be impregnated with calcium carbonate.

Face of hand or leg—surface between dorsal and ventral margins.

Finger—the movable finger of hand is the dactyl; the immovable or fixed finger, a projection of the propodus.

Fissure—cleft made by splitting or separation of parts with narrow opening.

Flagellum (plural: *flagella*)—whip-like multiarticulate appendage; terminal portion of antennule or antenna.

Foliaceous—leaf-like.

Foramen (plural: *foramina*)—aperture, or hole.

Front—part of carapace between orbits of eyes when no rostrum developed.

Fringe of setae—dense row of setae on margins.

Gape in hand—if the teeth of the fingers do not mesh a *gape* occurs.

Gastric region or area—median part of carapace.

Gonads—sex organs; ovaries or testes.

Gonopod—pleopod of male modified for copulation.

Gonapore or *genital pore*—small opening in integument through which eggs or sperm are released.

Granules and *granulate*—small prominences, like grains, making surface rough.

Groove—channel or hollow.

Gutter—shallow trough.

Hair—soft setae.

Hand—*chela* (plural: *chelae*)—propodus and dactylus of cheliped.

Hepatic region or *area*—part of carapace covering liver.

Hermaphrodite—having characteristics of both sexes; both male and female reproductive organs in one individual.

Hinged spines—movable spines.

Hooked bristles—stiff setae with curved tips; used to anchor camouflage materials on some spider crabs.

Horns—elongate protuberances; on the rostrum of spider crabs or the antennae of deepwater burrowing shrimps.

Host—the animal supporting a parasite or a commensal species..

Hydroid—a soft-bodied, marine animal.

Intestinal region or *area*—part of carapace covering intestine.

Integument—skin, or outer covering, of an animal.

Interbranchial region—area between branchial regions.

Invaginated—spines and setae of prezoea are like the fingers of a glove in which the tips have been pushed inwards.

Iridescence—showing colours like those of a rainbow and which change colour with position.

Ischium (plural: *ischia*)—3rd article or segment from attachment of pereiopod.

Keel—elevated ridge or carina.

Knob—rounded protuberance.

Lanceolate—shaped like a spearhead; tapering to each end.

Lamina or *laminate*—a thin plate or layer; a scale or flake.

Lateral—side; either side of a midline.

Linear—in a straight line.

Liparid—of a family of marine fishes.

Lithodid—crabs of the Family Lithodidae.

Littoral—of the shore; intertidal and shallow-water subtidal.

Mandibles—paired calcified jaws at mouth and concealed by mouth appendages.

Mantle—thin envelope of tissue enclosing body of some molluscs.

Maxillipeds—outer, or 3rd pair of maxillipeds are appendages anterior to pereiopods and usually cover mouth parts.

Maxillae—paired appendages in front of maxillules.

Maxillules—paired appendages in front of mandibles.

Median—midline of body or other structures.

Megalopa—last larval stage in development of crabs and other reptants.

Membranous—covered with a pliable sheet-like tissue.

Merus (plural: *meri*)—4th article, or segment, from body of appendage.

Molar-like teeth—grinding teeth on fingers or mandible.

Movable spines—spines with basal socket.

Mouth parts—paired appendages in front of mouth; mandibles, maxillules, maxillae and maxillipeds.

Multi-articulated—many-jointed.

Natatory—swimming.

Nauplius—larvae of some Crustacea; having three pairs of head appendages functional.

Neotenous—attainment of functional sexual maturity while otherwise immature.

Nodule—small rounded knob.

Notch—V-shaped indentation of margin or convex surface.

Ocular—pertaining to the eye.

Operculiform—having a plate or valve-like appendage.

Orbit—eye-socket; cavity on anterior carapace containing eye.

Orbital—region bordering orbit.

Ovate—egg-shaped.

Ovigerous—bearing eggs; also called berried.

Palm—propodus or hand without fingers.

Palp—feeler; jointed sense organ.

Papillate tubercle—small, nipple-like protuberance.

Parasite—organism which lives in or on another organism and obtains nourishment from the host.

Pedal disc (or *basal disc*)—flattened surface of a sea anemone used for attachment to substrate.

Pediform—foot-like appendage.

Peduncle—stalk or stalk-like process.

Pelagic—of the open sea.

Pentagonal—five-sided.

Pereiopods—paired thoracic appendages used for seizing food and/or locomotion.

Pigment—colouring matter.

Pincer—prehensile claw of Crustacea; a grasping organ.

Pinnate—branched in a feather-like manner.

Plankton—forms of life which inhabit surface layers of water; predominately drifting species; pelagic.

Platelets—minute flat surfaces which can reflect light.

Pleopods—abdominal appendages, paired or single, which may occur on first five segments, or be missing, especially in males; serve for swimming and/or a deposit for fertilized eggs in females.

Pleuron (plural: pleura)—lateral downward extension on abdomen in shrimps and shrimp-like Crustacea.

Plumose setae—feather-like; may serve as a net to catch floating food or for swimming.

Pointed granules—pointed knobs with sharp tips.

Pollex—immovable finger, fixed finger, or thumb on propodus of cheliped.

Polychaete—a segmented marine worm.

Posterior—at or near hind end of body.

Postero-lateral—posterior side.

Prehensile—describes a specialized appendage used for grasping or seizing.

Pre-ocular—in front of eye-socket.

Prezoea—last embryonic stage of decapod Crustacea.

Projection—protruding part.

Propod or propodus (plural: propodi)—6th article or segment from body of appendage.

Proximal—near; opposite to distal.

Pterygostomian area—triangular space on either side of buccal cavity in crabs.

Pubescent—having a soft velvet-like mass of setae.

Punctate—surface dotted with small holes.

Pyriform—pear-shaped.

Quadrate—square or rectangular.

Ramus (plural: rami)—branch.

Rasp—specialized setae on last two pairs of walking legs and on uropods of hermit crabs.

Reptant—able to crawl.

Reticulate—appearance of a network.

Rhizocephala—parasitic barnacles.

Ridge—line of junction where two sloping surfaces meet.

Rostral horns—rostrum divided into two elongated parts in some spider crabs.

Rostrum—"a beak"; a forward projection of carapace, between the eyes in Crustacea.

Rudimentary—an incompletely developed condition.

Rugose—wrinkled or corrugated.

Scale—overlapping plates, or article on peduncle of antenna and eyestalk.

Scaphocerite—antennal scale.

Segmented—divided into parts.

Semicircular—half a circle or a sphere.

Serrate—having a saw-like edge.

Sessile—fixed tightly to substrate and usually not capable of moving; sedentary.

Seta (plural: *setae*), *setose*—hair-like or needle-like structure on exoskeleton; bristles, setaceous, setiferous, and setigerous (terms used).

Shield—anterior calcified portion of carapace of hermit crabs.

Simple—not compound, nor divided into parts.

Sinus—a space or cavity in the body.

Somite—segment of body.

Spat—larval stage of oyster when first settled on substrate.

Sp. (plural: *spp.*)—is the abbreviation of species; often used when species has not yet been named.

Spatulate—racket (raquet)-shaped.

Spermatophore—capsule containing sperm.

Spherical—globular; shaped like a sphere.

Spine, spinous—sharp projection, some needle-like; spiny, spiniform.

Stalked—supported on a slender stem or stalk.

Sternum—ventral plates of body segments.

Stria and *striation*—linear marks on surface; may be slight ridges or furrows.

Styliform—shape of a style; ancient writing implement.

Stylocerite—spine or rounded lobe on side of base of antennule.

Stylambis—*appendix interna* of pleopod.

Sub—as a prefix-near, subequal, almost equal; i.e subchelate: resembling a chela, but with thumb missing or short.

Suborbicular—somewhat circular.

Subquadrate—almost square or rectangular.

Substrate—ground or other solid object to which an animal may be attached.

Sulcus (plural: *Sulci*), *Sulcate*—grooved or channelled.

Supraorbital—above orbit.

Suture—seamlike articulation of two parts; junction.

Symbiosus—a constant association between two different species of organisms.

Symmetrical—object which can be divided into two parts equal in size and shape.

Tail fan—sixth segment of abdomen, telson and uropods; used in swimming in some species.

Tooth, teeth—tooth-shaped projections.

Telson—terminal segment of abdomen, with anus opening ventrally.

Tergum (plural: *terga*)—dorsal surface of abdomen; separates pleura.

Tests—shell, or hard covering, of animals such as ascidians and sea urchins.

Thorn—spiny process.

Thumb or *pollex*—fixed finger of hand; a projection of propodus.

Tridentate—margin with three teeth.

Tubercles, tuberculate—small, rounded or sharp, projections.

undulated—wavy.

Uniramus—single-branch as compared to biramus or two-branched.

Uropods—modified pleopods of sixth segment of abdomen and part of tail fan; may be used in swimming or for holding hermit crabs within their shell.

Ventral—underside; opposite to dorsal.

Vermiform—worm-like.

Vestigial—degenerate, or of little use; a remnant of well-developed ancestral article.

Visceral fold or *skirt*—internal organ of horse clam *Tresus capax*.

Walking legs—pereiopods 2-5.

REFERENCES

BANNER, A. H. and D. L. MCKERNAN. 1943. A Record For *Emerita analoga* from the Washington Coast. Science, 97:119.

BARR, N. 1973. Extension of the known range of the crab. *Cryptolithodes typicus* Brandt. To Amchitka Island, Alaska (Decapoda, Anomura). Crustaceana, 25(3):320.

BUTLER, T. H. 1959. A record of the Anomuran Crustacea *Emerita analoga* (Stimpson) from British Columbia. J. Fish. Res. Board Can., 16(5):761

———— 1961. Records of decapod crustacea from British Columbia. Can. J. Zool. 39:59–62.

BUTLER, T. H. and J. F. L. HART. 1962. The occurrence of the King Crab *Paralithodes camtschatica* (Tilesius), and of *Lithodes aequispina* Benedict, In British Columbia. J. Fish. Res. Board Can., 19:(3):401–408.

BUTLER, T. H. 1967. A bibliography of the Dungeness Crab, *Cancer magister* Dana. Fish. Res. Board Can. Tech. Pap. 1:12 pp.

CHACE, F. A., JR. 1951. The oceanic crabs of the genera *Planes* and *Pachygrapsus*. Proc. U.S. Nat. Mus., 101(3272):65–103.

———— 1966. Decapod crustaceans from St. Helena Island, South Atlantic. Proc. U. S. Nat. Mus., 101(3536):622–662 (Oceanic crabs 646–647).

EFFORD, I. E. 1967. Neoteny in sand crabs of the genus *Emerita* (Anomura, Hippidae). Crustaceana, 13(1):81–93.

FAXON, W. 1895. Reports of an exploration off the west coasts of Mexico, Central and South America, and off the Galapagos Islands, in charge of Alexander Agassiz, by the U.S. Fish. Commission Steamer *Albatross,* during 1891, Lieut. Commander Z. L. Tanner, U. S. N. Commanding, XV. The stalk-eyed Crustacea. Mem. Mus. Comp. Zool. Harvard, 18:292 pp. *(Calastacus stilirostris* Faxon. 106–107, pl. 27).

FOREST, JACQUES ET MICHÉLE DE SAINT LAURENT. 1981. La morphologie externe de *Neoglyphea inopinata,* espèce actuelle de Crustacé Décapode Glyphéide. In: Rés. Camp. MUSORSTOM. I Philippines (18–28 mars 1976), Vol. 1, 2. Mém. ORSTOM, vol. 91, pp. 51–84, fig. 1–28.

GARTH, J. 1958. Brachyura of the Pacific Coast of America. Oxyrhyncha. Allan Hancock Pacific Exped., 21:854 pp.

GREBENYUK, L. P. 1975. Two new species of the Superfamily Thalassinidea. Zoologicheskii Zhurnal, 54(2):298–303.

HAIG, J. 1960. The Porcellanidae (Crustacea Anomura) of the eastern Pacific. Allan Hancock Pacific Exped., 24:440 pp.

HAIG J., T. S.HOPKINS AND T. B. SCANLAND. 1970. The shallow water Anomuran crab fauna of southwestern Baja California, Mexico. San Diego Soc. Nat. Hist. Trans., 16 (2):13–32.

HAIG, J. AND M. K. WICKSTEN. 1975. First records and range extensions of crabs in California waters. Bull. South. Calif. Acad. Sci., 74(3):100–104.

HART, J. F. L. 1940. Reptant decapod crustacea of the west coasts of Vancouver and Queen Charlotte Islands, British Columbia. Can. J. Res. Sect. D, 18:80–105.

———— 1959. A new distributional record for oceanic crabs. Ann. Rept. Prov. Mus. of Nat. Hist. and Anthrop, Victoria, British Columbia, 1958:31.

———— 1962. Records of distribution of some Crustacea in British Columbia. Ann. Rept., Prov. Mus., Nat. Hist. and Anthrop, Victoria, British Columbia, 1961:17–19.

———— 1963. Oceanic crabs found off the coast of British Columbia. Can. Field Nat., 77(2):127 pp.

———— 1965. Life history and larval development of *Cryptolithodes typicus* Brandt (Decapoda, Anomura) from British Columbia. Crustaceana, 8(3):255–276.

———— 1968. Crab-like Anomura and Brachyura (Crustacea: Decapoda) from southeastern Alaska and Prince William Sound. Nat. Mus. Can. Nat. Hist. Papers., 38:6 pp.

———— 1971. Key to planktonic larvae of families of Decapod Crustacea of British Columbia. Syesis, 4:227–234.

———— 1971. New distribution records of reptant Decapod Crustacea, including descriptions of three new species of *Pagurus,* from the waters adjacent to British Columbia. J. Fish. Res. Board Can., 28:1527–1544.

HART, J. F. L. 1980. New records and extensions of range of reptant Decapod Crustacea from the northeastern Pacific Ocean. Can. J. Zool., 58(5):767–769.

HOSIE, M. J. AND T. F. GRAUMER. 1974. Southern range extension of the Baird Crab *(Chionoecetes bairdi* Rathbun). Calif. Fish and Game, 60(1):44–47.

KOZLOFF, E. N. 1974. Keys to the marine invertebrates of Puget Sound, the San Juan Archipelago and adjacent regions. Univ. Wash. Press, Seattle: 226 pp.

MCGINITIE, G. E. 1935. Ecological aspects of a California marine estuary. Am. Mid. Nat., 16(5):717–718.

MCKAY, D. C. G. 1931. Notes on the Brachyuran Crabs of Northern British Columbia. Can. Field Nat., 45(6):187–189.

———— 1932 An additional Brachyuran Crab from northern British Columbia. Can. Field Nat., 46(7):153.

MCLAUGHLIN, P. A. 1963. Survey of the benthic invertebrate fauna of the eastern Bering Sea. Spec. Sci. Rept. U.S. Fish Wildlife Serv., 401:75 pp.

———— 1974. The hermit crabs (Crustacea Decapoda, Paguridea) of northwestern North America. Zool. Verh. Rijksmus. Nat. Hist. Leiden 130:396 pp.

MAKAROV, V. V. 1938. Crustacea, Anomura. *In:* Fauna of U.S.S.R. 10(3):1–289. (Translated from Russian by Nat. Sci. Found. Jerusalem, 1962).

———— 1941. The decapod Crustacea of the Bering and Chukchi Seas. Invest. Far East Seas U.S.S.R., 1:111–163 (in Russian; English Summary).

MENZIES, R. J. 1948. A revision of the brachyuran genus *Lophopanopeus.* Allan Hancock Found. Occas. Pap., 4:45 pp.

ODENWELLWER, D. B. 1972. A new range record for the umbrella crab, *Cryptolithodes sitchensis* Brandt. Calif. Fish and Game, 58(3):240–241.

PEARCE, J. B. 1966. The biology of the mussel crab, *Fabia sub-quadrata,* from the waters of San Juan Archipelago, Washington. Pac. Sci., 20(1):3–35.

Peden, A. E. and C. A. Corbett. 1973. Commensalism between a liparid fish, *Careproctus sp.* and the lithodid box crab, *Lopholithodes foraminatus.* Can. J. Zool., 51(5):555–556.

Pemberton, G. S., M. J. Risk and D. E. Buckley. 1976. Supershrimp: deep bioturbation in the Strait of Canso, Nova Scotia. Science, 192(4241):790–791.

Pereyra, W. T. and M. S. Alton. 1972. Distribution and relative abundance of Invertebrates off the northern Oregon coast, Columbia River Estuary and adjacent ocean waters. Bioenvironmental Studies, Univ. Wash. Press, Seattle, 444–474.

Rathbun, M. J. 1902. Descriptions of new decapod Crustaceans from the west coast of North America. Proc. U.S. Nat. Mus., 24:885–905.

———— 1904. Decapod Crustacea of the northwest coast of North America. Harriman Alaska Expedition, 10:210 pp.

———— 1918. The grapsoid crabs of America. Bull. U.S. Nat. Mus., 97:444 pp.

———— 1925. The spider crabs of America. Bull. U.S. Nat. Mus., 129:613 pp.

———— 1930. The cancroid crabs of America of the families Euryalidae, Portunidae, Atelecyclidae, Cancridae and Xanthidae. Bull. U.S. Nat. Mus., 152:609 pp.

———— 1937. The oxystomatous and allied crabs of America. Bull. U.S. Nat. Mus., 166:278 pp.

Saint Laurent, de M. 1972. Un Thalassinide du golfe de Gascogne, *Calastacus laevis* sp. nov. Remarques sur le genre *Calastacus* Faxon. (Crustacea Decapoda Axiidae). Bull Mus. nat. Hist. Paris (ser. 2, Zool), 29(35):347–356.

———— 1973. Sur la systématique et la phylogénie des Thalassinidea: définition des familles des Callianassidae et des Upogebiidae et diagnose de cinq genres nouveaux (Crustacea Decapoda). C. R. Acad. Sci. Paris: t. 227, ser. D.:513–516.

Schmitt, W. L. 1921. The marine decapod Crustacea of California. Univ. Calif. Publ. Zool., 23:470 pp.

SCHMITT, W. L. 1965. Crustaceans. Univ. Michigan Press. Ann Arbor. 204 pp.

SCHMITT, W. L., J. C. MCCAIN AND E. S. DAVIDSON. 1973. Crustaceorum Catalogus, pt. 3 Decapoda I, Brachyura I, Fam. Pinnotheridae. Dr. W. Junk. The Hague: 160 pp.

SHIINO, S. M. 1964. On three Bopyrid Isopods from California. Rep. Fac. Fish. Prefect. Univ. Mie 5(1):19–25.

SQUIRES, J. J. AND A. J. G. FIGUERIA. 1974. Shrimps and shrimplike Anomura (Crustacea Decapoda) from southeastern Alaska and Prince William Sound. Publ. Biol. Oceanogr. Nat. Mus. Can. (6):23 pp.

STEVENS, B. A. 1925. Hermit crabs of Friday Harbour, Washington. Publ. Puget Sd. Biol. Sta. Univ. Wash., 3:273–309.

———— 1927. *Orthopagurus,* A new genus of Paguridae from the Pacific Coast. Publ. Puget Sound Biol. Sta., Univ. Wash., 5:245–252.

———— 1928. Callianassidae from the west coast of North America. Publ. Puget Sound Biol. Sta., Univ. Wash., 6:315–369.

VINOGRADOV, L. G. 1947. Decapod Crustaceans of the Sea of Okhotsk. Rep. Pacific Res. Inst. Fish and Oceanog. 25. In Russian. F.R.B. English translation, no. 477.

WELLS, W. W. 1928. Pinnotheridae of Puget Sound. Publ. Puget Sound Biol. Sta. Univ. Wash., 6:283–314.

GENERAL REFERENCES WITH SECTIONS ON CRABS

HARBO, R. M. 1980. Tidepool and Reef, Marinelife guide to the Pacific Northwest Coast. Hancock House. North Vancouver: 56 pp.

JOHNSON, M. E.and H. J. SNOOK 1927. Seashore animals of the Pacific Coast. McMillan, New York: 659 pp. (Paperback reprint with original pagination, Dover, New York, 1967.)

LIGHT'S MANUAL. 1975. Intertidal Invertebrates of central California. Eds. R. I. Smith and J. T. Carlton. University of California Press, Berkeley. 716 pp.

MORRIS, R. H., D. P. ABBOTT AND E. C. HADERLIE. 1980. Intertidal Invertebrates of California. Stanford University Press. 690 pp.

RICKETTS, E. F. AND J. CALVIN. 1968. Between Pacific Tides. 4th edition, revised by J. W. Hedgepeth. Stanford University Press. 614 pp.

INDEX

263

264

ALSO IN THIS SERIES

* No longer in print.

For more information about these and other publications of the British Columbia Provincial Museum write or telephone:

PUBLICATIONS
British Columbia Provincial Museum
Victoria, British Columbia
V8V 1X4

Phone (604) 387-3701

M50-113